OBJECTIVE

IELTS

Michael Black
Wendy Sharp

Workbook

Intermediate

CAMBRIDGE
UNIVERSITY PRESS

CAMBRIDGE
UNIVERSITY PRESS

University Printing House, Cambridge CB2 8BS, United Kingdom

Cambridge University Press is part of the University of Cambridge.

It furthers the University's mission by disseminating knowledge in the pursuit of education, learning and research at the highest international levels of excellence.

www.cambridge.org
Information on this title: www.cambridge.org/9780521608732

© Cambridge University Press 2006

First published 2006
10th printing 2015

A catalogue record for this publication is available from the British Library

ISBN 978-0-521-60873-2 Workbook
ISBN 978-0-521-60874-9 Workbook with Answers
ISBN 978-0-521-60882-4 Student's Book
ISBN 978-0-521-60885-5 Self-study Student's Book
ISBN 978-0-521-60872-5 Teacher's Book
ISBN 978-0-521-60881-7 class cassette set
ISBN 978-0-521-60880-0 CD (audio) set

Cover design by Dale Tomlinson

Designed and produced by Kamae Design, Oxford

Contents

Communicate!

Reading

1 Skim the following text to find out answers to these questions.

1 What is it about?
2 Who are the main characters?
3 Where do you think the text is taken from? Give reasons for your answer.
   A a research paper
   B a newspaper article
   C a book about wildlife

⏱ about 350 words

N'Kisi knows what he's talking about

2 Scan the text again and answer the following questions.

1 Where does N'Kisi live?
2 What can he do that other parrots can't?
3 What else, besides speaking, have African greys been known to do?
4 How many words does Aimee Morgana think N'Kisi knows?
5 How old is N'Kisi?
6 What has the parrot had difficulty doing?

3 In the IELTS Reading Module, you won't be allowed to use a dictionary. It's important that you try to guess the meaning of words you aren't sure of. The following words are taken from the article. Look at the words in context and try to think of another word or phrase which means the same. When you have finished, check your answers in an English-English dictionary.

EXAMPLE: mastered (line 4) .... *learnt* ....

1 a running commentary (line 7) ....
2 to mimic (line 9) ....
3 making up (line 12) ....
4 cognitive powers (line 17) ....
5 to carry out (line 20) ....
6 complex (line 20) ....
7 chipped in (line 30) ....
8 linguistic conventions (line 39) ....

Squawking 'Pretty Polly' just isn't enough for some parrots. N'Kisi is able to hold a conversation. The African grey parrot, living in New York, has a vocabulary of almost 1,000 words and has mastered
5 basic grammar and sentence construction. He is able to ask for food and attention, but is far happier keeping up a running commentary on what is going on around him and talking to anyone who comes close.

African greys are well known for being able to mimic
10 human speech, but N'Kisi is believed to be the first to develop this ability into creating his own language. Owner Aimee Morgana has recorded him making up sentences 15 words long. The bird, according to her, takes into account past, present and future tenses.

15 Professor Donald Broom of the School of Veterinary Medicine at the University of Cambridge, who is an expert on the cognitive powers of animals, said that the parrot's conversational abilities should not cause too much surprise. African greys are intelligent birds
20 and can be taught to carry out complex tasks, like completing jigsaws when the pieces fit into shaped holes. They can also respond to circumstances, such as by saying 'good night' when you turn the lights off at night or 'goodbye' when you put a coat on.

Ms Morgana, an artist with an interest in animal 25 behaviour, believes N'Kisi's vocabulary is in the region of 972 words. But she is more impressed by the comments he comes out with, such as when she was picking up the beads of a necklace from the floor and N'Kisi chipped in 'Oh no, you broke your 30 new necklace.'

The six-year-old bird is also able to recognise different objects, shapes and colours and describe what he sees. When he first met Dr Jane Goodall after seeing a picture of her with one of the 35 chimpanzees she studies, the parrot asked 'Got a chimp?' Seeing another parrot hanging upside down, N'Kisi called out 'You got to put this bird on the camera.' However, some linguistic conventions have proved difficult for the parrot. While trying to put 'fly' 40 into the past tense, he said 'flied' instead of 'flew', just as young children often do.

Grammar

The passive

G ···⫶ STUDENT'S BOOK page 138

4 Scan the article again and find two examples of the passive.

5 Complete this chart of past forms. It contains both regular and irregular verbs from Unit 1 of the Student's Book.

Infinitive	Past tense	Past participle
send	*sent*	*sent*
take		
teach		
make		
form		
be		
spend		
find		
say		
use		
speak		
give		

6 Complete the sentences below using one of the verbs from exercise 5. Some verbs may be used more than once. Think carefully about which tense to use – you may need to use a modal passive with *can*.

EXAMPLE: The information about the Internet survey *was sent* to households last week.

1 Progress .... (recently) on plans for the new IT building.
2 Last year, more money .... on new computer terminals than on anything else in the department.
3 It .... that more research is needed into whether mobile-phone masts are dangerous to health.
4 Latin .... (very rarely) nowadays.
5 Grey parrots .... to speak.
6 When you enrol next Tuesday, you .... more details of the course.
7 Ice .... when the temperature of water is below freezing point.
8 Information on a range of subjects .... on the Internet.

Vocabulary

7 Complete this puzzle of words to do with communication by solving the clues below. The number of letters in each word is given in brackets. What word appears vertically?

1, 2 It is very common to send a .... to a friend these days. (4, 7)
3 N'Kisi has learnt to .... (4)
4 The Principal will give a .... at the end of term. (6)
5 In order to be heard, you need to .... clearly into the microphone. (5)
6 I often call my friends to have a .... about college. (4)
7 It's good to have someone you can .... a conversation with. (4)
8 Give me a .... sometime, and we'll arrange to go out somewhere. (4)
9 If you want to attract someone's attention from a distance, you can always .... (7)

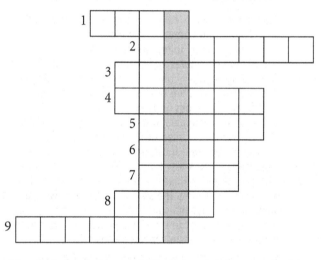

8 Match the verbs (1–8) with the correct nouns (a–h) to form collocations to do with communication.

1	tell	**a**	a question
2	whistle	**b**	a foreign language
3	ask	**c**	an answer
4	speak	**d**	advice
5	offer	**e**	surprise
6	make	**f**	a tune
7	have	**g**	a lie
8	express	**h**	a speech

A healthy diet

Reading

1 Quickly read this article about fast food.
Time yourself as you read.

⏱ about 580 words

FAST FOOD –
behind the image

We all know what a fast-food outlet looks like and what it serves. This is because when a big modern business offers fast food, it knows that we, its customers, are likely to want No Surprises. We are hungry, tired and not in a
5 celebratory mood.

The building itself is easy to recognise and designed to be a 'home from home', on the motorway or in the city. However, the usual things you find in a restaurant are a little different – tables and chairs are bolted to the floor,
10 and cutlery is either non-existent or not worth stealing. Words and actions are officially laid down, learned by the staff from handbooks and teaching sessions, and then picked up by customers in the course of regular visits. Things have to be called by their correct names
15 (cheeseburger, large fries); the staff have a script they must learn – you know the sort of thing: 'Will that be with cheese, sir?', 'Have a nice day' – something I find particularly irritating. The staff wear a distinctive uniform, menus are always the same and even placed in the same
20 spot in every outlet in the chain; prices are low, and the theme of cleanliness is repeated endlessly.

The company attempts to play the role of kind and concerned parent. It knows people are suspicious of large corporations and so it tries to stress its love for children; it
25 often has cottagey-style buildings for warmth and cosiness or large glass walls and smooth surfaces to show cleanliness and modernity. It responds to social concerns, but only if beliefs are sufficiently widely held and

therefore 'correct'. Take, for example, the worry about fat in our diets. Fast-food chains only responded by putting 30
salad on the menu when there was pressure in various countries from doctors and health ministers. Some chains are busy at present showing how much they care about the environment, too.

Fast-food chains know that they are ordinary. They want 35
to be ordinary and to be thought of as almost inseparable from the idea of everyday food consumed outside the home. They are happy to allow their customers time off for holidays – Thanksgiving, Christmas and so on – for which they do not cater. Even those comparatively rare 40
holiday times are turned to a profit because the companies know that their favourite customers – families – are at home together then, watching television, where carefully placed commercials will spread the word concerning new fast-food products and re-imprint the 45
image of the various chains for later. Families are the customers the fast-food chains want; good, law-abiding citizens who love their children, teaching them how good hamburgers are for them. The chains even have very bright lighting to make sure that 'undesirable' people 50
don't want to come in.

Supplying a hamburger that is perfect in terms of shape, weight, temperature, together with selections from a pre-set list of extras, to a customer who knows what to expect, is a difficult thing to do. The technology involved 55
has meant spending huge sums on research, and there are also political and economic questions to consider – how to maintain supplies of cheap beef and cheap buns. However, the image that is maintained is of a 'casual' eating experience. Make up your own mind, but there's 60
more to a hamburger than just beef in a bread roll.

2 Do the following statements agree with the information given in the reading passage? ⋯⟩ TF1

Write

TRUE   if the statement agrees with the information
FALSE   if the statement contradicts the information
NOT GIVEN   if there is no information on this

EXAMPLE: Customers often choose to eat in fast-food outlets because they know what to expect. *TRUE*

(See underlined text.)

1 Each employee is encouraged by the chain to have his/her own individual way of communicating with customers.
2 Fast-food companies started selling salads because of worries about health.
3 Salad is one of the more popular choices at certain fast-food outlets nowadays.
4 Fast-food companies want to attract people who are too busy to cook at home.
5 There are certain types of customers who are not welcome at fast-food outlets.
6 Supplying hamburgers to customers is very straightforward.
7 More money needs to be spent on research into new fast-food technology.

Grammar

Comparatives and superlatives

(G) ···❖ STUDENT'S BOOK page 138

3 Make sentences, using a comparative adjective and other necessary words.

EXAMPLE: Mount Everest / Mount Kilimanjaro – a lot / high
Mount Everest is a lot higher than Mount Kilimanjaro.

1 the River Nile / the River Thames – considerably / long
2 London / Mexico City – far / small
3 fruit / sweets – much / good
4 Rolls Royce car / bicycle – a good deal / expensive
5 fast food / cooking yourself – more / convenient
6 Australia / New Zealand – far / big

4 What can you say about the following things?

EXAMPLE: the Pacific Ocean
It's the biggest ocean in the world.

1 the Sahara Desert   4 Pluto
2 the Great Wall of China 5 redwood tree
3 Bill Gates   6 the cheetah

5 These sentences contain errors made by IELTS students. Correct them.

1 Fast-food outlets are open longer that ordinary restaurants.
2 I would rather have a sandwich then a pizza.
3 The number of people who eat rice is considerably greater the number who eat potatoes.
4 The amount of meat eaten in the USA is far more that eaten in China.
5 Hamburgers are more popular as noodles in Europe.
6 Pizza is not so expensive than steak.
7 Producing meat is twice expensive in some countries than in others.
8 The number of customers we had today was much few as last night.

Vocabulary

6 Look at the clues and find the words in the wordsearch. The number of letters is in brackets. The words go vertically and horizontally. (↓→)

1 Indian food is often like this. (5)
2 If you leave milk for a long time, it will go like this. (4)
3 I prefer to eat bread which is like this. (5)
4 Too many of these aren't good for your teeth. (6)
5 Bananas are like this when they are yellow. (4)
6 What you do when you want to lose weight. (4)
7 The person who does the cooking. (4)
8 Food which has no taste is like this. (5)
9 Fish and chips and burgers are this. (4, 4)
10 You look at this when choosing your meal in a restaurant. (4)

A	L	K	R	E	M	E	N	U	P
S	P	I	C	Y	N	C	S	K	R
N	F	A	S	T	F	O	O	D	I
M	Q	F	W	A	Q	L	T	T	P
L	R	R	D	S	S	O	U	R	E
D	I	E	T	N	W	D	C	V	N
S	H	S	T	Y	E	I	C	D	E
V	H	H	E	Z	E	G	H	H	J
C	M	Q	G	N	T	A	E	F	R
B	L	A	N	D	S	X	F	C	M

7 Complete the table with the other forms of the words given. Take care with spelling. Use an English-English dictionary to help you.

Noun	Adjective	Adverb	Verb
1	hungry	2	3
4	celebratory		5
6	distinctive	7	8
cleanliness	9	10	11
12	suspicious	13	14
warmth	15	16	17
cosiness	18	19	
20	21	comparatively	22
23	political	24	25

3 City attractions

Reading

1 The four paragraphs below describe the cities shown in the photographs. Skim the text quickly. Can you match each photograph to the appropriate paragraph and identify the cities?

⏱ about 430 words

A Although there aren't many historic sites to attract tourists, this is a fascinating city. It's a major business centre, and its port is one of the busiest in the world. A construction boom that began in the early 1990s means there are now a large number of high-rise buildings. In January 2004, an exciting new transport link went into service – 'maglev' trains (using magnetic levitation technology) run between the city centre and the international airport, reaching a speed of 430km per hour. A traditional garden in the Old City contains a teahouse that may be the model for the well-known 'willow pattern' design, which is used on plates around the world.

B This city was probably founded in the 16th century and is laid out in a grid – that is, most of its streets are straight, like lines drawn on a sheet of paper from top to bottom and from side to side. One very impressive avenue is 140m across and is said to be the widest in the world. The main government building is called *la Casa Rosada*, which is Spanish for 'the Pink House'. One of the main attractions for tourists is watching – or even dancing – the tango. The hottest months of the year are January and February.

C This city was founded in the early 18th century to increase trade by sea with western Europe. A lot of canals were excavated, which made it resemble the city of Venice. As a result, this city is often called 'the Venice of the North'. Between 1712 and 1918, it was the country's capital. Although its name was changed to Petrograd and Leningrad in the past, it is again known by its original name. One of the famous attractions in this city is the Hermitage, an art gallery largely located in the Winter Palace. It contains an amazing collection of paintings.

D This ancient, historic city is over 2,600 years old. It was first called Byzantium and then Constantinople before adopting its present name. It's on both sides of a narrow stretch of water separating the two continents of Europe and Asia. There's plenty to interest and amuse tourists, so they need never get bored! Topkapi, the magnificent palace, used to have over 50,000 people living and working in its grounds, and even had its own zoo. Another impressive building is the Grand Bazaar, the largest indoor market in the country, with more than 3,000 shops and restaurants. It used to be the commercial centre of the city and is usually crowded with both tourists and local people.

2 Complete these notes. The notes come in the same order as the relevant part of the passage. Choose NO MORE THAN ONE WORD from the passage for each answer. ⋯⫶ TF3

City A

EXAMPLE: There is a great deal of activity in this city's ....*port*.......... .

1 A large amount of .... has taken place in recent years.
2 Very fast .... connect the city with its airport.

City B

3 Most streets in this city form a ....
4 'The Pink House' is used by the ....
5 A popular dance in this city is the ....

City C

6 Like Venice, this city contains a large number of ....
7 This city used to be the .... of the country.
8 Many people visit a palace here to see the impressive display of ....

City D

9 The two parts of this city are located in different ....
10 There used to be a zoo in the grounds of a ....
11 The Grand Bazaar is a covered ....

3 The passage contains four paragraphs labelled A–D. Which paragraph contains the following information? You may use any letter more than once. ···⟩ TF7

EXAMPLE: a similarity between this city and another one. ...*C*

1 a description of how roads are arranged ....
2 the possibility that famous representations may be of a building in this city ....
3 a reference to activities that no longer take place in a certain building ....
4 the reason for establishing this city ....
5 a potential disadvantage for the tourist industry ....
6 a reference to a name that has come back into use ....

Vocabulary

4 Find the word in the reading passage that matches each definition. The definitions are in text order.

1 a large increase, particularly in economic activity ....
2 in a style that has continued for a long time without changing ....
3 an object or person that is represented by an artist ....
4 brought into existence, set up ....
5 a pattern of horizontal and vertical lines crossing each other to form squares ....
6 dug (a hole or channel in the ground) ....
7 look or be like something else ....
8 in a particular place ....
9 choosing as its own ....
10 dividing into parts ....

5 Complete each sentence with the word from the box that best suits the meaning. More than one answer is possible in some cases. Pay attention to any preposition after the space.

amazed	amused	astonished	bored	excited
fascinated	frightened	interested	surprised	
terrified	thrilled			

1 I saw a cat trying to catch fish in the canal, and I was so .... I started laughing.
2 I thought Helen was on the other side of the world, so I was .... to see her in Shanghai.
3 Takuya is very .... in the history of Topkapi Palace, so he has bought a book about it.
4 Juan has got the whole day free, but he can't think of anything to do, so he's ....
5 The side of the bridge had been damaged, and Brad was .... that a child might fall into the river.
6 Tania was .... with her prize of a round-the-world trip, because it was something she'd always dreamed of.
7 Hasan couldn't take his eyes off the people dancing in the street, he was so .... by them.
8 The band gave such a fantastic performance that the crowd became more and more .... , and started dancing and cheering.

Grammar

Cause, purpose and result

 **G** ···⟩ STUDENT'S BOOK page 138

6 Complete each sentence with one of the words or phrases in the box.

because	because of
so that	so

1 Shanghai doesn't have many historic attractions, ... not many tourists realise what an interesting city it is.
2 There are now a great many high-rise buildings in Shanghai .... the recent construction boom.
3 An old teahouse in Shanghai is a popular place to visit .... it might have inspired the famous 'willow pattern' design.
4 The main government building in Buenos Aires has been painted pink, and .... it is now known as *la Casa Rosada* – the Pink House.
5 A lot of people visit Buenos Aires .... they can learn the tango.
6 The weather is warmest in Buenos Aires in January and February .... the city is in the southern hemisphere.
7 The site of St Petersburg was chosen .... ships could sail between the city and western Europe.
8 St Petersburg is known as 'the Venice of the North' .... its canals.
9 Istanbul is over 2,600 years old, ... it is much older than St Petersburg.
10 The Grand Bazaar in Istanbul attracts plenty of tourists .... the large number of shops and restaurants it contains.

4 Ways of learning

Grammar

Present tenses

G ···> STUDENT'S BOOK page 139

1 Look at these sentences. Most of the verbs in **bold** contain errors which are typical of those made by IELTS candidates. Put a line through the wrong words and write the correct ones. One sentence is completely correct.

> EXAMPLE: Those people who ~~are taking~~ part in sports like scuba diving usually ~~spends~~ a lot of money. _take, spend_

1 Service-oriented companies often **giving** mobile phones to their sales force. ....
2 I **am writing** to tell you that I **become** a full-time student. I started my course last week. ....
3 Since I was a child, I **want** to be a nurse. ....
4 The table **is showing** that the number of students **is rising** to over five million since 1980. ....
5 We **don't see** each other for a long time, so I **want** to meet soon. ....
6 I **want** to be an engineer. This is the reason I **have decided** to go to college. ....
7 In this way, I feel I **am being** able to repay the hours and effort that **have been spent** on me. ....
8 In the past decade, computers **are becoming** the most useful tool in offices and factories. ....
9 This letter is to tell you what I **doing** recently. ....
10 This development **is being happening** for many years. ....

2 Complete this passage by using the correct present tense in each space. One verb should be in the passive. There is an example to help you.

Ever since I was a child I **0** (love) _have loved_ piano music, though until recently I never had the chance to play myself. But at last I **1** (start) .... having lessons at the adult education college in my town. It was hard at first, but Sarah, my teacher, says that now I **2** (make) .... good progress.

I'm a computer programmer, and usually **3** (work) .... long hours, so I **4** (not have) .... much spare time. I **5** (practise) .... several times a week, but unfortunately the piano **6** (belong) .... to my neighbours, so I only **7** (play) .... when it's convenient for them. Now I **8** (think) .... about buying my own piano, so that I can play whenever I **9** (like) ....

Every year, there's a concert at the college, and some of the music students **10** (ask) .... to perform. Recently I **11** (practise) .... a piece by Shostakovich, and I **12** (hope) .... I'll be good enough to play it in the next concert.

Sarah **13** (suggest) .... that I take a piano exam next year, but I **14** (not decide) .... yet. It **15** (depend) .... on whether I can afford to buy a piano for myself.

Prepositions

3 Prepositions are normally followed by a noun, pronoun, *-ing* form or *wh-* word. They can't be followed by any other verb forms. Look at these sentences, based on the recording in 4.1 of the Student's Book (page 26). Complete each sentence with a preposition from the box.

about	at	from	on	to	with

Preposition + noun or pronoun
1 We've been looking .... different forms of education.
2 I don't really look forward .... English lessons.
3 What about your future career – have you thought much .... it?

Preposition + -ing

4 My parents thought I could cope .... being taught at home.

5 Apart .... working on projects, what subjects do you study?

6 I'm thinking seriously .... becoming a doctor.

Preposition + wh- word

7 My mother and I talk .... what exactly the project should cover.

8 In my next project, I want to focus .... why some people choose one-to-one education for their children.

4 These sentences include errors that are often made by IELTS candidates. Put a line through the wrong words and write the correct ones. One sentence is correct.

EXAMPLE: I'm interested in ~~find~~ out about the people who live in my town.
...*finding*...

1 Writing a project takes a lot of read. ....

2 Let's talk to what you've done. ....

3 I'm interested from finding out about people's jobs.
....

4 I've been thinking about what you said. ....

5 How do you feel about use a computer? ....

6 I'm looking forward to start a new project. ....

7 I'm quite good to find information on the Internet.
....

8 I enjoy most lessons, apart of history. ....

9 Children are usually better at learn foreign languages than adults. ....

10 Next, we'll look to the best way to plan a report.
....

Reading

5 This passage is similar to Section 2 of General Training Reading. Read it quickly, timing yourself as you read.

⏱ about 300 words

Southmoor College – Policies and Procedures

The College has introduced a number of policies and procedures which are briefly summarised here. A leaflet containing full details is available on request.

■ The College Charter is a series of statements which explain what is being done to promote high standards for people who use College services. It has been designed in accordance with a national framework aimed at maintaining and improving standards, while at the same time being tailored to meet the specific needs of the College.

■ Formal complaints should be submitted in writing to the Principal, who will refer each complaint to the appropriate member of staff and then provide a response.

■ The College has developed both informal and formal appeals procedures in connection with its own internal examinations. Appeals against external examination bodies must follow their own procedures, and details are available from the Examinations Officer.

■ The College is a designated No Smoking Area. Smoking is not permitted inside any part of the building unless specifically authorised.

■ All accidents must be reported to Reception as soon as possible and the appropriate form completed.

■ Students are responsible for the apparatus, tools or machinery with which they are working. If items are damaged or broken as a result of careless use or failing to follow instructions, the person concerned will be required to cover the cost of repairing or replacing the items. All equipment must be left in a clean state and in good working order.

■ Mobile phones are part of everyday life, but they must be used with consideration for other people. Please ensure that you have switched them off before entering classrooms or the library. They must not be taken into any examination room under any circumstances.

6 Do the following statements agree with the information given in the passage? ┄⟩ TF1

Write

TRUE   *if the statement agrees with the information*
FALSE   *if the statement contradicts the information*
NOT GIVEN *if there is no information on this*

1 Anyone wishing to see the complete policies and procedures should ask for them.

2 The Charter was written after consultation with groups of people who use the College.

3 The Charter is identical to the charters of the other colleges in the country.

4 Replies to formal complaints will be given by the Principal.

5 The College's appeals procedure applies to all examinations taken in the College.

6 Smoking inside the College is allowed in certain circumstances.

7 The College can provide medical help if an accident occurs.

8 Students may have to pay for equipment that they break.

9 Mobile phones can be taken into examination rooms if they are switched off.

5 Discovering the past

Vocabulary

1 Match these people (1–10) to their field of study (a–j).

EXAMPLE: archaeologist *someone who studies the physical remains of the past*

1	biologist	**a**	someone who studies animal and plant life
2	botanist	**b**	someone who studies the basic characteristics of substances, including their reactions
3	economist	**c**	someone who studies the past
4	mathematician	**d**	someone who designs buildings
5	paediatrician	**e**	someone who helps clients who have legal problems
6	anthropologist	**f**	someone who is interested in the consumption and production of goods and services
7	architect	**g**	someone who studies number, shape and quantity, among other things
8	historian	**h**	someone who specialises in children's diseases
9	lawyer	**i**	someone who studies human beings, their customs and relationships
10	chemist	**j**	someone who specialises in plant life

2 What are these shapes?

EXAMPLE: *circle*

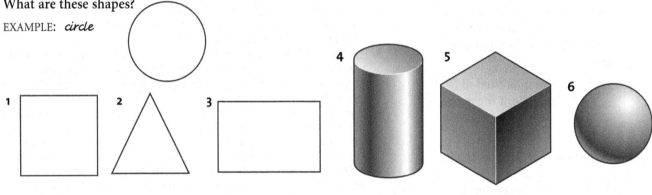

1 .... 2 .... 3 .... 4 .... 5 .... 6 ....

3 Look at these sets of words. Which is the odd one out and why? Use an English-English dictionary to help you.

1 circle   square   triangle   rectangle
2 cylinder   cube   sphere   circle
3 enormous   tiny   huge   vast
4 average   medium   minute   standard
5 sizeable   immense   minuscule   colossal

4 Complete each sentence below using a verb from the box in the appropriate form.

analyse	carry out	evaluate	make
perform	put forward	reach	support

1 Dr Jones .... the conclusion that the bones weren't 5th century.
2 After .... the analysis, they found that the people had come from Polynesia.
3 The test results .... at the laboratory.
4 The builders who .... the discovery were given a reward.
5 Our findings .... Professor Rice's theory.
6 After .... the statistics, Peter decided to publish them.
7 The person who .... the experiment on the bones was Stephen Doughty.
8 No one has yet officially .... the theory that the city inhabitants died of starvation.

Grammar

Past tenses and sequencing

G ⋯⫶ STUDENT'S BOOK page 139

5 Put the verbs in brackets in the most suitable past tense.

EXAMPLE: Last year, I (join) ......*joined*...... a dig in Egypt.

1 When I arrived at the museum, everyone (go) .... home and the place was empty.
2 Zara and Ali (arrive) .... early at the hotel before the others and (eat) .... immediately without waiting for anyone else to arrive.
3 They (pass) .... the Chinese exhibit when something about it (catch) .... their eye.
4 I (not enjoy) .... studying Economic History when I was at college.
5 Anna was in the library all evening and so (miss) .... seeing the film.
6 I (work) .... on my coursework when I (see) .... that I (make) .... a huge mistake and would have to start again.
7 I (see) .... my tutor in the city centre yesterday, but he (not see) .... me – he .... (talk) to his wife.
8 The tourists (climb) .... the path to Machu Picchu when there was a sudden thunderstorm overhead.
9 Before entering the tomb, the archaeologist (make) .... a speech.
10 While I (dig) .... the trench, I (cut) .... my hand.

6 Read through these sentences about some new research. Put them in the right order and provide punctuation.

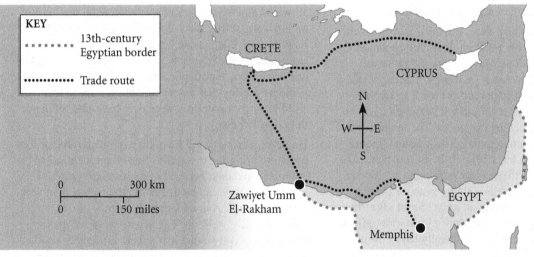

a ...*1*... it has been known for a long time that the ancient egyptians imported copper from cyprus
b .... the fortress was only needed for a brief period only 50 years or so and was abandoned in the 13th century bc
c .... the men grew their own food and baked bread but imported luxury items such as wine and olive oil
d .... the fortress was built around 1270 bc by rameses II to protect maritime trade
e .... the complex covered five acres and was home to at least 500 soldiers
f .... new research carried out by a team from liverpool university has shown how the egyptians built a huge fortress on this coast
g .... it was 20 metres long and ten metres wide with three central rooms
h .... as well as a bakery and a palace a temple was also discovered
i .... what historians had not realised until recently was the threat posed to these imports by aggressive tribesmen along the mediterranean coast

What is job satisfaction?

Reading

1 Read the text below about how people may choose their career and say where this text is taken from.

A a scientific conference journal
B a newspaper article about a new book
C a textbook on motivation at work

⏱ about 600 words

The Douglas family

Meet Bernard Shapiro. He is a friendly 64-year-old and the Principal of McGill University, in Canada. He's an extremely tidy person and listens to opera. Before he accepted his current job, he worked as a statistician.
5 Many of the same things could be said of Harold Shapiro, Bernard's identical twin. He's also a former statistics expert and an opera lover with a taste for order in the workplace. And he is President of Princeton University in the USA. Both seem a little taken aback
10 by the way their lives have followed a similar pattern. 'It never occurred to me – or, I believe, to my twin – to deliberately plan similar careers,' Bernard says.

Easily the strangest thing about Principal and President Shapiro, though, is how far from unusual they actually
15 are. For they are just one of many pairs of twins to feature in a major new work by Professor Nancy Segal that provides the most important evidence so far that career choice, working style and job satisfaction can be significantly influenced by our genes. The implications
20 reach far beyond identical twins. The headline finding in her study is that at least 30% of the factors that make an individual choose their career path could be genetic. 'I'm not saying that there is a single gene for being a carpenter or a gene for being an artist,' Segal says, 'but
25 our studies do suggest that the choice of any job reflects many characteristics that are genetically based, from physical size to personality.'

Her evidence is clear enough. It is based on studies of career parallels between identical twins – including,
30 importantly, many who have been brought up separately – and twins who are non-identical, or fraternal. Identicals, who usually share 100% of genes, showed a far greater degree of similarity in their working lives than fraternals, who typically share an average of 50%.
35 'We're not in the occupations we have by accident,' she says. 'I'm a teacher and researcher, and I could probably have been a clinical psychologist. But I couldn't have been an investment banker or plumber.'

Career dynasties are nothing new – there are the tycoon Murdochs, film star Douglases and political Churchills, 40 all well-known examples of a phenomenon that occurs in any walk of life. But the idea that there might be more to such coincidences than parental pressure and a ready-made set of contacts just waiting to be networked has some important implications. Not least among them 45 is the possibility that parents intent on forcing their child towards a specific career may have less influence than they believe.

However, Professor Val Dusek is sceptical. 'One of the problems with this research is that when identical twins 50 are raised together, because of their striking physical similarities, they can be treated by their parents in very particular ways. And as for all the stories of coincidences – well, one can often find some quality between any two people that appears strangely similar.' 55

A much less controversial but arguably more significant finding from Segal's research is the idea that job satisfaction may also be in the genes. Furthermore, Segal's results suggest that job satisfaction seems to play a much greater role than expected. Employers take 60 note: changing the lighting or the seating arrangements, providing free coffee or even increasing salaries may not contribute to their employees' happiness as much as giving them meaningful and personally satisfying goals. So, whatever it is that motivates an actor to endure the 65 poverty of lengthy 'resting' periods in return for the occasional bit of acting, or a lecturer to tolerate poor pay in order to pursue his or her academic passion, may be buried deep in their ancestry.

2 Complete each sentence with the correct ending A–G below. ⋯⟩ TF3

1 Professor Nancy Segal
2 An employer
3 A parent

A has clear evidence to show that there is a gene for particular jobs.
B needs to rethink his or her strategy for motivating the workforce.
C will try to bring up each twin as a separate individual.
D believes that a third of people choose a career because of their genes.
E is less likely to be the most important factor in their child's choice of job than previously thought.
F has shown that people don't choose a job by chance.
G concludes that some jobs are harder than others.

3 Do the following statements reflect the claims of the writer? ⋯⟩ TF1

Write

YES   *if the statement reflects the claims of the writer*
NO   *if the statement contradicts the claims of the writer*
NOT GIVEN *if it is impossible to say what the writer thinks about this*

1 The Shapiros were a bit surprised when they found that they had both chosen the same career.
2 It is unusual to find twins who have both reached high positions.
3 Families who follow the same career are usually limited to specific fields.
4 Parents can help their child find a job by talking to people they know.
5 Professor Val Dusek believes Segal's research is correct.
6 People sometimes find their career disappointing.

Grammar

Past simple or present perfect?

G ⋯⟩ STUDENT'S BOOK page 139

4 Complete each sentence with the verbs in brackets, using either the past simple or present perfect.

EXAMPLE: Over the years, many famous people (follow) *have followed* in the footsteps of their parents.

1 Unemployment (not rise) .... for the past two years.

2 I (be) .... a doctor for ten years now.
3 Lisa (study) .... chemistry at school and then (go) .... on to college.
4 My brother (ring) .... me one morning and (say) .... he (have) .... a job in Australia.
5 Tom (never be) .... a hard worker – he prefers to stay in bed in the morning.
6 I (see) .... a career adviser two years ago.
7 My cousin (enjoy)........................ her job ever since she was promoted.
8 We (spend) .... many years building up our business before we retired.

5 Complete the sentences with the correct tense of the verbs in brackets and with *for, since* or *ago*.

EXAMPLE: I (not see) *haven't seen* him *since* 1999.

1 I (last see) .... Michael Douglas in a film five years ....
2 One actor I know (not work) .... many years and he still isn't working.
3 Peter (have) .... a holiday three months ....
4 Val Dusek (be) .... sceptical about the book ever .... it was published.
5 When Sue (teach) .... in Zambia eight years .... , she (not enjoy) .... it.
6 Paul (not had) .... a job .... the past year.
7 We (last go) .... on a marketing trip four weeks ....
8 I (learn) .... French at school, many years ....
9 'How long (you be) .... manager of the company?' '........................ 2003.'

Vocabulary

6 Find ten verbs that collocate with *money* in this wordsearch. (→↓)

C	H	A	N	G	E	Z	P
A	L	E	N	D	I	S	A
T	L	S	Q	U	N	P	Y
L	E	A	V	E	V	E	M
Y	S	V	Y	L	E	N	A
T	R	E	M	J	S	D	K
W	A	S	T	E	T	P	E
T	N	F	G	I	V	E	D

7 Selling dreams?

Reading

1 In the General Training and Academic Reading Modules, you may be asked to match questions to short texts or sections of a longer text. Read these web pages, A–D, which advertise various events and organisations. Then read the sentences below and decide which advertisement each one refers to. Write the correct letter A–D next to each question. ⋯⋗ TF2

⏱ about 430 words

A

Nathan's Famous
International Hot-Dog Eating Contest

The preliminary ceremonies of this famous annual competition will begin at 11.30 a.m., with bands, rappers and children's chorus. 12.25 p.m. sees the introduction of this year's eaters, who represent nations from all over the world, and at 12.40 p.m., the historic 12-minute all-you-can-eat contest will begin. Will anyone beat the world record, which stands at over 50 hot dogs and buns in 12 minutes?

Viewing is available on a first-come-first-served basis. Television crews are invited to use a two-tiered stage 3m from the main stage. The area in front of the main stage is reserved for still photographers and television cameras without tripods.

B

fröjeL vikiNg Re-eNactmeNt society

Few periods in history stimulate the imagination as much as the era when the Vikings were known – and sometimes feared – throughout Scandinavia, the British Isles, Russia, all the Mediterranean, Africa and even America. Fröjel (pronounced Fro-yel) is a family-based Viking re-enactment society depicting the Vikings from a harbour that was one of the richest trading centres in the Viking world – Fröjel, on the Swedish island of Gotland.

The members' aims are to re-create the clothing, weapons, tools, jewellery, games, food and furniture of that long-gone period, and enjoy an escape to a simpler, more relaxed time, with like-minded people. We will also use the items we have made by reliving that age at various public entertainments.

C

Drive a steam engine!

Now anyone can be an engine driver! Join us for a day's introductory course, during which you will learn the basic techniques of driving a 60-year-old steam locomotive, under the eye of an experienced instructor. Then, why not try the advanced course, giving you first-hand experience of operating a locomotive? Lunch and refreshments are provided on both courses at no extra cost. You are also given one-year membership of the railway society, which gives you the opportunity to become a volunteer on our educational programme.

D

The Wedding Fair

One of the most popular events in the Barnwell Centre's annual programme, the Wedding Fair, takes place every March and September. As well as displays from leading suppliers of wedding dresses, caterers, photographers and many more, a wide range of specialists will be on hand to give expert advice on planning your wedding.

The full programme of events includes a fashion show, which features wedding outfits for brides, grooms, bridesmaids and page boys. The Great Hall is decorated to show how it could look for your wedding reception. Refreshments are available in our self-service restaurant.

1 The charge for attendance includes food. ....
2 You will be able to take part in displays for others to watch. ....
3 This event takes place once a year. ....
4 You will be taught certain skills. ....
5 Participants have the opportunity to see clothes being modelled. ....
6 Spectators will have the chance to listen to musical entertainment. ....
7 If you pay for an activity, you are automatically enrolled in this organisation. ....
8 Facilities are provided for the media. ....
9 Participants make copies of everyday objects from the past. ....
10 Information is available about organising an event. ....

Grammar

Relative clauses

G ···❖ STUDENT'S BOOK page 139

2 In the advertisements above there are six relative clauses introduced by *who*, *which* or *that*. Underline those words, and decide whether the clauses are defining or non-defining.

3 There are two other forms of *who*: *whose* (the possessive form, similar to *my* and *his*) and *whom* (which normally follows a preposition). The passage that follows is part of an article about advertising techniques. For each space, choose the right word from the box. In some cases, there is more than one possibility. There is an example to help you.

that	which	who	whom	whose

How advertisers make you buy

Are you one of those people **0** ....*whose*.... expenditure is greater than their income? If so, read on – you might find out why you spend so much on goods **1** .... you don't really need.

One of the most common techniques with **2** .... advertisers try to persuade you to buy their products is for a person **3** .... name and face you know well to tell you that they can't live without that particular product. These celebrities, most of **4** .... can hardly need the money **5** .... they receive for it, may endorse the most unexpected products – like the footballer **6** .... appeared in an advertising campaign for packets of snack food.

Another common style is the advert in **7** .... we're told that everybody else has already bought the product, so you'd better hurry if you don't want to be the one person **8** .... doesn't have it. This high-pressure approach generally works because it's difficult for you to find out whether or not the product is really selling well. You have to take the advertiser's word for it, **9** .... means you're at their mercy. Adverts using this technique often tell us to 'hurry while stocks last' or give the date when the 'special offer' ends.

4 Relative pronouns can be omitted when they are the object in a defining relative clause:

The advertising is about the benefits (which/that) we hope to gain.

In the passage in exercise 3, the relative pronoun can be omitted from two spaces. The first one is number 1. Which is the other one?

5 The relative pronoun and the verb *be* are often omitted in front of the *-ing* and past participle forms of verbs and in front of adjectives. Put a line through those that can be omitted.

EXAMPLE: The agency ~~which is~~ running the fruit juice campaign is a very small company.

1 The new commercial for fruit juice, which was first shown on TV last month, has led to a jump in sales.
2 The advertising agency that was responsible for the fruit juice campaign won an award.
3 Newspapers, which first appeared in England around 1622, transformed advertising.
4 Adverts that were missing from early newspapers were ones for household goods.

Vocabulary

6 Answer these questions with phrases from the advertisements on page 16. Each answer contains an adjective made up of two or more words joined with hyphens.

EXAMPLE: Which words describe the length of a competition? *the 12-minute contest*

Which words ...
1 mean people who share similar interests?

   ....

2 describe the way in which places are allocated to spectators? ....
3 refer to a period of belonging to an organisation?

   ....

4 mean that you do something yourself?

   ....

5 refer to a place where you collect and eat food?

   ....

6 explain what happens in a competition?

   ....

7 suggest the different ages of people who belong to an organisation? ....
8 give something's age? ....
9 mean a time that has finished?

   ....

Apart from the hyphen, what other difference is there between *12 minutes* and *(the) 12-minute (contest)*? One of your answers should follow the same rule: which one?

8 Time to waste?

Grammar

Talking about the future

(G) ⤳ STUDENT'S BOOK page 140

1 Complete this letter, using the verbs in brackets with *will* (*'ll*), *going to*, present simple or present continuous. As this is an informal letter to a friend, use contractions, like *'ll* and *'m*.

The future can be seen in different ways, so there are usually several ways of talking about a future event. However, in this exercise, express the meanings given in the notes on the right. This will help you to remember the differences between the various ways of expressing the future.

Dear Sarah

How **1** (you celebrate) .... your birthday next month? If you haven't arranged anything, do come to a concert by the orchestra I've just joined. We **2** (play) .... music by your favourite composer, and I'm sure you **3** (not regret) .... it, as we're pretty good!

The concert **4** (be) .... on a public holiday, and the tickets are already selling very fast, so clearly it **5** (be) .... a sell-out.

My only problem is that the performance **6** (start) .... quite late — at 9 p.m. — and I **7** (fly) .... to the West Indies the following day. The plane **8** (leave) .... early in the morning, so it **9** (be) .... quite a rush! I **10** (not spend) .... the next few weeks worrying about it though.

Do come — it **11** (be) .... great to see you. I **12** (send) .... you a leaflet about the concert as soon as they're available.

Love
Jenny

1 already decided
2 already arranged
3 prediction
4 timetable
5 result of something in present
6 timetable
7 already arranged
8 timetable
9 prediction
10 already decided
11 prediction
12 making a decision

2 These three passages were written by IELTS candidates. Correct the errors in the phrases in bold. Four of them are already correct.

Dear Friend
This letter is to invite you to my grandmother's birthday party. It's a special occasion, because my grandmother **1 is going to be** 100 years old. I've decided to give her a big surprise, so **2 I'll make** dinner. The dinner **3 is** on 1st July at seven o'clock in the Hacienda Club, and the night **4 would begin** with a favourite song of my grandmother's.

Dear Helen
Do you remember that in my hurry to travel back home, I left a big suitcase in your basement? Would you please send it to me and tell me the cost of shipment? **5 I'm going to pay** you back as soon as possible.

There is much controversy nowadays about whether the radio **6 will continue** to exist or not. Some people claim that the radio **7 will use** for a very long time. Those who disagree argue that TV and the Internet create a lot of problems. Some people spend all their spare time watching TV or playing on the Internet, and by doing this they **8 will waste** a lot of time which they could spend with their family or friends. But I firmly believe that reasonable use of the TV and Internet and keeping the radio are very important and necessary. Decreasing the negative effects of all the media **9 will to make** our society more secure than before. Otherwise, they **10 will have** a bad impact on our way of life.

3 Rewrite the part of each sentence in italics, using the words in brackets and keeping as close as possible to the sentence given. Don't change the meaning.

1 *Maybe there will be another opportunity* to go to a rock concert next month. (may)

....

2 I'm looking forward to the outdoor concert, and luckily *the weather promises to be fine.* (likely)

....

3 Jill and Dave see every play at the local theatre, so *I'm convinced they'll be there tonight.* (bound)

....

4 So many people want to see this musical that *you're unlikely to get tickets.* (probably)

....

5 Our performance was so good that *we may win the drama competition.* (chance)

....

6 *I doubt whether* many people will go to see a play in a foreign language. (unlikely)

....

7 *We probably won't* have time to go to the show. (little chance)

....

8 *This is definitely* one of the best exhibitions we have seen locally. (no doubt)

....

Reading and grammar

4 Read the article below about the history of juggling. Ignore the spaces. Choose the best heading for each paragraph from the list below. ⋯⋗ TF4

1 Paragraph A ....
2 Paragraph B ....
3 Paragraph C ....
4 Paragraph D ....
5 Paragraph E ....

⏱ about 325 words

List of Headings

i Recent discoveries
ii The end of a form of entertainment
iii Join a juggling class!
iv Anyone can try it
v Jugglers as celebrities
vi The technical demands increase
vii Different functions in different regions
viii Jugglers get organised
ix Audiences expect more from jugglers

A short history of juggling

A The history of juggling can be traced back 4,000 years to paintings of female jugglers **1** .... the walls of Egyptian tombs. In ancient civilizations in India, China, Japan, Iran and Central America, some form of ball manipulation was associated **2** .... religious rituals. Through the Middle Ages in Europe, juggling was practised only by wandering entertainers and court musicians.

B After several centuries when juggling was not recorded, it surfaced again in England in 1819. **3** .... the late 19th century, jugglers had become well established in the variety theatre in Europe. The best of them were incredibly creative and skilful, fully deserving the star status they achieved. Paul Cinquevalli, for instance, juggled an umbrella, a top hat and a bottle of water tied at the top with paper. He ended the act **4** .... tossing the hat to his head, opening the umbrella above him and throwing the bottle so that its open end stuck on the point of the umbrella, cascading water over the umbrella and all around him!

C In the late 1920s and 1930s, radio and talking movies attracted audiences away **5** .... live performances. Hundreds of small-time jugglers had filled the variety theatres, but few of them survived the death **6** .... those venues.

D Times were tough **7** .... jugglers through the 1940s, 50s and 60s. In the USA, some of them formed the International Jugglers Association in 1947. Through a newsletter and annual conventions, they communicated, sharing juggling tricks and tips on good locations for performing.

E In the 1970s, juggling became a craze in California, with teenagers taking **8** .... the streets and beaches to perform. Some were politically motivated, but most were just youngsters looking **9** .... a way of earning a little money. The kids who started on the street began a process that has removed juggling from the exclusive domain of the circus and nightclub and turned it **10** .... an approachable endeavour for everyone.

5 Now read the article again, and choose one of these prepositions for each space. You will need to use some of them more than once.

by	for	from	into	of	on	to	with

Climate change

Reading

1 Scan the text for the following information.

1 When did drilling begin?
2 How big are the pieces in which the ice cores are stored?
3 How many ice ages do the ice cores show?
4 Without global warming, how long would it be before we had another ice age?

⏱ about 500 words

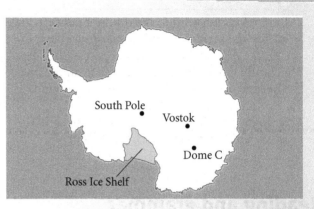

Drilling ice cores in Antarctica

Antarctica is both beautiful and very remote, being 2,700km from Australia and 3,500km from Africa. It is one-and-a-half times the size of Europe and is covered by a layer of ice up to 4,700m thick in places. Scientists
5 from ten European countries have been drilling into the ice since 1996, as part of the European Project for Ice Coring in Antarctica (EPICA).

An ice core is produced by a drill cutting through the ice and retrieving a cylinder of ice. These ice cores are
10 stored in slices 10cm in diameter and 3m long. When they first come out of the ground, they are at a temperature of −50°C. They are then kept until they reach −20°C when they are ready to be analysed in laboratories around the world.

15 Scientists find the ice cores invaluable because they contain tiny bubbles of air which were trapped when snow turned into ice. This air is being analysed to see how much carbon dioxide and other greenhouse gases, such as methane, have been present in the atmosphere
20 over many hundreds of thousands of years. Results show that the levels of methane and carbon dioxide are much higher today than in the past.

The deepest ice cores have been drilled at a site known as Dome C, where the East Antarctic ice sheet is about
25 3.4km thick. The ice sheet here is one of the most inhospitable places on Earth with average surface temperatures of −54°C. At an altitude of 3,233m above sea level, Dome C is so cold and dark for much of the year that the scientists can only carry out drilling for
30 two out of every 12 months.

At Dome C, the deepest and oldest ice core yet drilled in the Antarctic suggests that the world's climate is heading for a period of abnormal weather conditions brought about by man-made greenhouse gases. Chemical analysis of the ice within the core has
35 revealed details of eight ice ages that have affected the Earth during the past 740,000 years. Scientists say that the present climate most closely resembles the warm 'interglacial' period about 470,000 years ago, but with the difference that this time temperatures are set to go
40 upwards as a result of global warming. Scientists from EPICA report that without the extra carbon dioxide being pumped into the atmosphere, it appears that our present climate would remain stable well into the future.

Some people have argued that human-induced global
45 warming is beneficial because it averts the next ice age. However, according to Eric Wolff of British Antarctic Survey, this is misguided. 'If the climate is left to its own devices,' he says, 'we would have about another 15,000 years to go before the next ice age. If people say
50 global warming is good because it stops us going into another ice age, they are wrong because we are not about to go into another ice age quite yet.'

2 Do the following statements agree with the information given in the article? ···⟫ TF1

Write

TRUE if the statement agrees with the information

FALSE if the statement contradicts the information

NOT GIVEN if there is no information on this

1 The ice cores need to warm up before they are sent to scientists.
2 Scientists have found similar levels of methane and carbon dioxide in the ice cores.
3 The previous ice ages were brought about by abnormal weather conditions.
4 Global warming is universally believed to be a bad thing for the Earth.
5 Eric Wolff believes there will be another ice age at some point in the future.

3 Which definition, a or b, best matches the following words or phrases as they are used in the text?

EXAMPLE: retrieving (line 9)
a (bringing out)   **b** saving

1 inhospitable (line 26)
  a unwelcoming   **b** unsociable
2 heading for (line 33)
  a starting at   **b** going in the direction of
3 brought about (line 34)
  a happened   **b** created
4 are set to (line 40)
  a are likely/certain to   **b** are programmed to
5 stable (line 44)
  a unchanged   **b** firm
6 averts (line 46)
  a prevents   **b** moves
7 misguided (line 48)
  a misunderstood   **b** mistaken

Grammar

G ···⟫ STUDENT'S BOOK page 140

Noun/verb agreement

4 The *Cambridge Learner Corpus* tells us that IELTS candidates find the agreement of verbs, nouns and determiners (*the*/*any*, etc.) difficult. Correct the following errors from IELTS scripts. There may be more than one error.

1 One of the factories near me are causing a lot of problems.
2 Many things worries me about what are happening to the environment.
3 Every things in the town were hidden in thick smog.
4 There is many advantage to using solar power.
5 A number of problem has arisen recently in low-lying towns.
6 Another thing to mention are that we need to plant more trees.
7 Every countries has problem with a lack of fossil fuels.
8 These thing is now being used to make all kind of products.
9 A lot of thing to remember are that children needs a safe world to grow up in.
10 All kind problem will happen if the government don't do something soon.

Countable and uncountable nouns

5 Complete the following sentences with *much*, *many*, *few* or *little*.

1 The sea level is rising. We haven't got .... time.
2 Very .... research was done on climate change before 1950.
3 'How much work have you done?' 'Very .... , I'm afraid.'
4 There isn't .... news from the project manager this week.
5 .... scientists are finding it hard to get funding these days.
6 How .... research activities are you involved in?
7 There's very .... accommodation available at the research station.
8 We haven't had .... good weather recently – very .... sunshine.
9 .... people have heard of the ice-core drilling project.
10 There's very .... time left before our climate changes for good.

Vocabulary

6 Unjumble these words to do with the environment.

EXAMPLE: UPTLLNIOO    P_ollution_

1 GDEREANEND PEECISS   E................... S...................
2 GCCYNLERI   R...................
3 LLBAGO GRWAIMN   G................... W...................
4 BOACNR XIODEID   C................... D...................
5 EENHGUSROE SSGEA   G................... G...................
6 CEI GAES   I................... A...................
7 IMTAECL EGACNH   C................... C...................
8 EAS EELVL   S................... L...................

A place to work or live in

Reading

⏱ about 550 words

HOW SKYSCRAPERS WORK

A
Throughout the history of architecture, there has been a continual quest for height. Thousands of workers toiled on the pyramids of ancient Egypt, the cathedrals of Europe and countless other towers, all striving to create something awe-inspiring. Although today people build skyscrapers primarily because they are convenient, ego and grandeur still sometimes play a significant role in the scope of the construction, just as they did in earlier times.

B
Up until relatively recently, however, builders could only go so high – the main obstacle being the downward pull of gravity. In order to build upwards, there has to be more material at the bottom to support the combined weight of all the material above. For example, if you increase the base of a pyramid, you can build it up indefinitely, but this becomes unworkable as the base would take up too much land. As a result, people didn't construct many buildings over ten stories.

C
But in the late 1800s, a number of advances and circumstances converged, and engineers were able to break the upper limit. In the USA, the social circumstances that led to skyscrapers were the growing metropolitan American centers, most notably Chicago. Businesses all wanted their offices near the center of town, but there wasn't enough space. In these cities, architects needed a way to expand the metropolis upward, rather than outward. The main technological advancement that made skyscrapers possible was the development of mass iron and steel production. New manufacturing processes made it possible to produce long beams of solid iron. Narrow, relatively lightweight metal beams could support a lot of weight, while taking up very little space. Then, with the advent of the Bessemer process, the first efficient method for mass steel production, architects moved away from iron to steel.

D
The central support structure of a skyscraper is its steel skeleton. Metal beams are riveted end to end to form vertical columns. At each floor level, these vertical columns are connected to horizontal girder beams. Many buildings also have diagonal beams running between the girders, for extra structural support. In a typical skyscraper substructure, each vertical column sits on a spread footing. The column rests directly on a cast-iron plate, which sits on top of a grillage. This is basically a stack of horizontal steel beams, lined side by side in two or more layers. The grillage rests on a thick concrete pad which is on the soil. Once the steel is in place, the entire structure is covered with concrete.

E
Once you get more than five or six floors in the building, you need to have something to move people up through the building quickly and efficiently. Skyscrapers would never have worked without the development of elevator technology. Ever since the first passenger elevator was installed in New York's Haughwout Department Store in 1857, elevator shafts have been a major part of skyscraper design.

F
Experts are divided about how high we can really go in the near future. Some say we could build a mile-high (1,609m) building with existing technology, while others say we would need to develop lighter, stronger materials before these buildings were feasible.

1 Read the article on page 22 from an American magazine. It has six paragraphs labelled A–F. Which paragraph contains the following information? ⋯⊱ TF 7

EXAMPLE: a necessary addition to tall buildings *E*

1 the way a tall building is constructed today *D*
2 the outlook for tall buildings *C F*
3 the emotional need for tall buildings *C A*
4 breakthroughs in building materials *C*
5 the disadvantage of old building techniques *B*

2 Label the diagram below. ⋯⊱ TF 10

A typical skyscraper substructure – (1) *steel skeleton spread footing*

(2) *metal beams (vertical column)*

Cast iron plate
(3) *horizontal girder beam spread footing*

(4) *grillage (steel beams)*

(5) *spread footing (thick) concrete pad*

soil

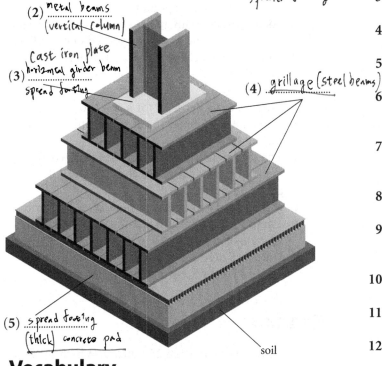

Vocabulary

3 The article on skyscrapers contains American English spelling and words, for example *center* for *centre* and *elevator* for *lift*. Match the American words in column A with the British words in column B.

A		B	
1	apartment *i*	a	post
2	train station *j*	b	cinema
3	drugstore *k*	c	garden
4	check *d l*	d	note
5	mail *a*	e	rubbish
6	fall *h*	f	sweets
7	candy *f*	g	maths
8	bill *d*	h	autumn
9	garbage *e*	i	flat
10	math *g*	j	railway station
11	backyard *c*	k	chemist's
12	movie theater *b*	l	bill

Grammar

-ing forms and infinitives

G ⋯⊱ STUDENT'S BOOK page 141

4 Complete the sentences below, using the correct form of the word in brackets and adding a preposition, if needed.

1 There's no point (decorate) ...., as I'm only living here for a couple of months.
2 We've decided (share) .... a house in the city centre.
3 Stephen can't stand (live) .... with untidy people.
4 Toni suggested (move) .... to New York.
5 Tina succeeded (buy) .... her dream house in Italy.
6 Pablo's parents made him (study) .... medicine instead of letting him (do) .... art history.
7 Repairing the roof now will involve (do) .... a lot of work in cold weather.
8 We put off (get) .... a new shower put in until December.
9 After (interview) .... several people, we couldn't decide who (ask) .... to move in.
10 Would you mind (open) .... the window for me?
11 The builder carried on (work) .... all evening.
12 Dr Fisher apologised (keep) .... the architect waiting.
13 Marco can't afford (leave) .... home yet.
14 We hope (move) .... soon (get away) .... from the neighbours.
15 I agreed (give) .... him £50 a month towards the electricity bills.
16 She stopped (smoke) .... in her room after her mother shouted at her.
17 Could you recommend somewhere (stay) .... when I'm in Paris?
18 Lisa was advised (study) .... architecture at college.
19 I want (go) .... to see the new art gallery tonight.
20 My dad's not very good (fix) .... things.

Animal life

Grammar

Articles

G ⋯⟶ STUDENT'S BOOK page 141

1 Read the passage below quickly. As you read it, decide which of these sentences best sums up what it is about.

A Some animals are more intelligent than some human beings.

B Research into animal behaviour is making us reassess our ways of measuring human intelligence.

C Some animals are able to learn from human beings.

D We are increasing our understanding of animal intelligence.

2 Read the passage again, and write *a, an, the* or nothing in each space.

Intelligent animals

It used to be thought that only 1 .... human beings were able to use 2 .... tools. In recent years, however, 3 .... research has shown that some animals have developed 4 .... same ability.

5 .... chimpanzees appear to be among the most intelligent animals, and 6 .... study of some living in 7 .... certain region of West Africa found that they use 8 .... crude stone tools to crack open 9 .... nuts when they are hungry. Even more surprisingly, perhaps, they teach 10 .... skill to their young. The chimps that were studied show precise control over the force needed to break open 11 .... nuts. They use enough pressure to crack them open, but not so much that they break into 12 .... very small pieces that cannot be eaten.

13 .... chimps select 14 .... heavy stones and carry them to where the nut trees grow, which is 15 .... sophisticated behaviour for 16 .... animal of any species. They collect their nuts, put them on 17 .... flat, horizontal piece of 18 .... wood and hit 19 .... nuts with 20 .... stones. Mothers show their young how to crack 21 .... nuts, just as 22 .... human beings teach their children.

3 The *Cambridge Learner Corpus* shows that IELTS candidates make a large number of errors with articles. These sentences, written by IELTS candidates, contain errors with the article. Those in **bold** are the wrong article or are used when there shouldn't be one. The spaces show where an article is missing. Correct the errors.

1 I expect you to send **a** people to repair the power supply.

2 I hope you are in **a** good health.

3 Today you may buy the latest car in the market, but in .... few weeks' time it will be outdated.

4 Some people believe that traditional skills are disappearing due to .... development of technology.

5 There is a big demand for **a** fast food.

6 I do a lot of hobbies in my spare time. Generally I listen to **the** music.

7 The experience gained from working when they are young will help these children to find .... good job much faster.

8 I wouldn't say that everywhere is .... same.

9 These two charts show **the** information about the sale of cars last year.

10 Unfortunately, we had **a** bad service when we went to your restaurant for dinner.

Reading

4 Read the article on page 25 quickly. Which of these is the main topic?

A the different abilities of various types of animals

B how some animals interact with other species

C differences between human and animal behaviour

⏱ about 375 words.

The social life of
mammals

5 The passage has four paragraphs labelled A–D. Which paragraph contains the following information? (You may use any letter more than once.) ···﹥ TF7

1 a reference to possible harmful effects of not knowing about other individuals
2 examples of what individuals need to know about connections between group members
3 a reference to human beings sharing a social skill with other mammals
4 what makes it possible for mammals to spend time growing up
5 how individual members of a species identify themselves
6 where knowledge is located in the individual
7 a contrast between the social organisation of mammals and of other species
8 a suggestion concerning a connection between length of childhood and the amount of learning the individual requires

A When it comes to social behaviour, mammals are far more highly developed than other creatures. Some birds may form pairs or even co-operate to hunt, but the complexity of their relationships can hardly compare to those within a group of dolphins, elephants or humans. What makes mammalian ⁵ social groups different from, say, a flock of starlings or a shoal of fish is that in many cases the individuals recognise each other. Although we may think that all elephants look pretty much the same, we can easily tell individuals of our own species apart, and it has become clear through studies ¹⁰ that the same is true of other species of mammals. Dolphins have their own signature whistles that act like names, and elephants can recognise and greet other individuals they have known but not seen for many years. This is something that only a few species of birds appear to be able to do. ¹⁵

B Mammals in complex social groups not only recognise each other as individuals, they also remember a lot of information about that individual. Social groups often rely on this memory – such as knowing who is dominant to whom, who is related to whom, and who has done what to ²⁰ whom in the past. They have to learn who to trust, who their friends are and who to watch out for.

C All this remembering goes on in a particular part of the brain called the neocortex. If you compare the size of a mammal's social group with the size of this part of the brain, you find ²⁵ they are remarkably closely related. This area, though, seems to take a long time to develop fully, and animals in which it is very large take a very long time to grow up to adulthood. During this time, the youngster has to learn all the rules of social behaviour in their group and to piece ³⁰ together all the relationships between the group members: knowledge that will be needed to avoid getting into trouble.

D Like all the advanced and specialised features that mammals have, social behaviour has developed because of the one defining characteristic that mammals possess: ³⁵ the production of milk, allowing baby mammals to have a period of childhood in which they can develop their own distinctive and successful characteristics.

6 Complete the summary below. Choose no more than ONE WORD from the passage for each answer. ···﹥ TF5

The social life of mammals

Mammals behave in a much more complex way than **1** .... or **2** ....
For example, **3** .... make individual sounds that distinguish them from each other.
4 .... are another non-human species that can remember individuals after a long absence.

Certain mammals retain **5** .... about individuals, partly because they need to know which ones they can **6** .... This memory is located in the **7** .... area of the brain. Animals in whom that part of the brain is large take a long time to reach **8** .... While they are growing up, they need to work out the social rules of their group and the **9** .... among its members. Mammals are only able to have a long period of growing up because they can be provided with **10** ....

Vocabulary

7 The adverbs in the box are used in the reading passage of 11.1 of the Student's Book or in this unit of the Workbook. Choose the best word to complete each sentence.

closely	eventually	hardly	highly
independently	respectively	relatively	
remarkably	simultaneously		

1 For a long time, very little was known about what animals do underground, but modern technology .... made it possible to film them.
2 .... , certain species of birds can make tools which they use to get access to food.
3 Dolphins and sharks are mammals and fish ....
4 When male frogs sing .... , they are more likely to attract females than if they sing alone.
5 Although elephants are .... harmless, it is unwise to go too close to them.
6 The development of social behaviour seems to be .... connected with having a long childhood.
7 Many nature programmes on TV are .... thought of.

Sport: just for fun?

Reading

about 450 words

1 You are going to read two short articles about using psychology to help athletes to improve their performance. Read the article below quickly, and as you read it, try to answer this question.

Which is the best summary of the writer's opinion?
A Sports psychology is of most use to athletes at the top of their field.
B The media give insufficient information about the value of sports psychology.
C Sports psychology is of great value to all athletes.
D Too much emphasis is placed on the usefulness of sports psychology.

about 125 words.

There's more to winning than just physical ability

Sports psychology involves preparing the mind of an athlete just as thoroughly as one prepares the body. For many top-level, professional, recreational and even youth athletes, successful performances cannot
5 simply be reduced to superior physical performance. Mental preparation includes setting clear, short-term goals, thinking positively, etc.

Thanks to the extensive media coverage of athletic events nowadays, the sports enthusiast can
10 understand the need for and benefits of sports psychology. Examples of mental training surround us; for instance, skiers, divers and gymnasts picturing their routines before they perform. Concepts such as motivation training and relaxation
15 are the basis for strong mental preparation, whether for a team or an individual sport, for an amateur or a professional, for a coach or an athlete.

2 Complete the sentences below with words taken from the passage above. Use NO MORE THAN ONE WORD for each space. ⋯⊱ TF3

1 Psychological preparation is just as important as .... preparation.
2 Athletes should decide on their .... for the near future.
3 Most people interested in sport are now aware of the .... for sports psychology.
4 Many athletes imagine their .... in order to improve their performance.
5 Basic mental preparation is useful for both .... and .... sports.

A Critical View of Sports Psychology Consultants

A good sports psychology consultant can be of great value for a sportsman or woman. However, after many years' experience, I have reluctantly come to the conclusion that a large number of these consultants –
5 that is, people claiming expertise in working with athletes on psychological aspects of competition in sport – fail to reach the required standard. Many professionals claim to be the key to improving a sportsman or woman's concentration, team
10 performance and virtually every other skill they require. They are interviewed in local and national newspapers and heard on radio shows, and a surprising number of professional teams use one. However, the opinion that I have reached in my experience as a sports psychology
15 consultant seems to be shared by many players, and not a few consultants: too many professionals in this line of work are not worth the money they cost. Because of the incompetence of these people, the idea has gained ground that working with a sports
20 psychology consultant is a mistake. Yet this should not be the general view, as a skilled consultant can make a major contribution to success in sport.

Several reasons can be identified for poor performance by sports psychology consultants. One is a tendency to
25 overvalue qualifications. Most consultants believe that their qualifications are the most appropriate and effective way to impress potential clients. I beg to differ. Numerous examples can be given of consultants who have the necessary skills without a certificate from a
30 sports psychology organisation. Many, too, are far more effective than some consultants with a qualification.

3 Skim the passage above, on the same subject, and answer this question.

Which is the best summary of the writer's opinion?
A Sports psychology is useful, but too many consultants are bad at their job.
B The media give a false image of the value of sports psychology.
C Sports psychology can never be of value to athletes.
D Few sportspeople realise how sports psychology could help them.

4 Scan the article again and answer this question.

What is the writer's job?
A sports psychology consultant
B athlete
C journalist

Another cause for concern is the number of consultants who lack the necessary skills or experience. Some sports psychology professionals work only on performance issues, and are unable to engage in individual counselling for personal, or life, issues, which is an essential aspect of the work. Others have plenty of clinical skills, but no idea how to help sportspeople to become more successful at sport. Most have neither the skills nor the expertise needed to help their clients get results. 35 40

Even if they have all the other skills required, most sports psychology consultants are inadequate because they lack the interpersonal skills needed to work effectively with their clients. I have seen consultants behaving very unprofessionally, for instance by guaranteeing results or becoming angry when faced with a client's decision to change to another consultant. 45

The bottom line is this: when choosing a sports psychology consultant, it is important to get information about them, for instance from past or present clients. Then it is possible to make an informed decision regarding hiring them. Clients should not be afraid to demand both quality and character; if they don't, plenty of money will be wasted. 50 55

5 Do the following statements agree with the views of the writer of the second article? ···⟩ TF1

Write

YES   *if the statement agrees with the views of the writer*

NO   *if the statement contradicts the views of the writer*

NOT GIVEN *if it is impossible to say what the writer thinks about this*

EXAMPLE: The media pay too much attention to sports psychology consultants. *NOT GIVEN*

(In lines 11–12, the writer mentions the media attention given to sports psychology consultants, but does not say that this is too much.)

1 Newspapers are responsible for the increasing demand for sports psychology consultants.

2 A number of sports psychology consultants overcharge their clients.

3 Qualifications are essential for a good consultant.

4 Consultants should help clients with both personal and performance issues.

5 Consultants should promise clients that their help will be successful.

6 Clients should only change consultants if they have a good reason.

7 It is useful to speak to people who have used a particular consultant before hiring him or her.

Grammar

should, had better, ought to

G ···⟩ STUDENT'S BOOK page 141

6 Decide which of the following each sentence is being used to do.

A give advice
B express probability

1 You shouldn't wear glasses during your bungee jump because they might fall off.

2 Recent evidence should convince doubters that the Aztecs played far more challenging sports than those we have today.

3 You want to become a champion? Then you should do a lot of practice.

4 The number of events in the Winter Olympics has increased in recent years, so there should be around 80 next time.

5 You're in peak condition, so you shouldn't have any problem completing the marathon.

7 These sentences were written by IELTS candidates. In each one, decide if the phrase in **bold** is used correctly or not, both in meaning and grammar. If not, correct it.

1 It is very cold these days, so I hope you **should take** care of yourself.

2 In my opinion, governments **shouldn't subsidise** bodies such as orchestras and drama companies.

3 People **should not to be encouraged** to take part in dangerous sports like scuba-diving or mountain-climbing.

4 It will be cold when you visit Shanghai, so you **had better to take** warm clothes with you.

5 We **not ought to spend** our time cooking dinner after working all day.

6 The fire was caused by old electric wiring, so I think we **had better ask** the landlord to replace it.

7 It is a little cold, so I think **it's better you bring** warm clothes and your boots.

13 Choices

Grammar

Conditionals

(G)···→ STUDENT'S BOOK page 141

1 Make conditional sentences from these situations.

  1 I can't decide. You have to help me.
    I can't decide unless ....

  2 Eating cheese makes me fat, so I don't eat it.
    If I don't eat cheese, ...

  3 I didn't go to Spain. I didn't learn Spanish.
    If I had gone to Spain, ...

  4 I'm unhappy. I have to make a lot of choices.
    I wouldn't be unhappy if ....

  5 I want to go to a good university. I will get a good job.
    As long as I go to a good university, ...
    ....

  6 I spend too much in restaurants. I need to learn to cook.
    If I learnt to cook, ...

  7 I went to a party last night. I woke up late this morning.
    If I hadn't been to a party last night, ...
    ....

  8 Nick can have the job, but he needs to learn to drive first.
    Nick can have the job as long as ....
    ....

  9 Susanna isn't here. She could help us.
    If Susanna were here, ...

 10 I was unhappy. I married the wrong man.
    I wouldn't have been unhappy if ....
    ....

Vocabulary

2 The following are important nouns which are often used in academic writing. Complete the sentences below using one of the words from the box.

analysis	evidence	factor	paper
process	research	source	theory

  1 Your .... of the situation is correct.

  2 His .... on 'Choice' was widely publicised.

  3 The .... of applying to college can be complicated.

  4 One .... in his promotion was his excellent research.

  5 Can you put a tick to indicate that you've read the research .... ?

  6 There is no .... of original ideas in this work.

  7 The .... of evolution was put forward by Darwin.

  8 In your bibliography, you must quote every .... that you use.

3 Form nouns from the words below. All the nouns occur in the passage in 13.1 of the Student's Book.

   1 satisfy   ....
   2 grow   ....
   3 able   ....
   4 politics   ....
   5 opt   ....
   6 tend   ....
   7 decide   ....
   8 expect   ....
   9 economise   ....
  10 differ   ....
  11 govern   ....
  12 recommend   ....

4 Find the nouns from exercise 3 in this wordsearch. (They are all singular.) (→↓)

D	T	H	E	O	P	T	I	O	N	R	E	I	S
I	O	N	L	G	O	V	E	R	N	M	E	N	T
F	Y	O	N	E	L	G	S	O	E	D	A	N	D
F	H	E	T	I	I	S	A	O	C	U	R	L	O
E	X	P	E	C	T	A	T	I	O	N	R	G	D
R	J	E	N	S	I	U	I	S	N	C	H	R	I
E	S	T	D	E	C	I	S	I	O	N	H	O	E
N	I	S	E	S	I	O	F	V	M	E	R	W	E
C	I	G	N	N	A	M	A	B	I	L	I	T	Y
E	A	Y	C	H	N	I	C	S	S	W	I	H	L
L	B	E	Y	D	O	N	T	E	T	I	N	H	E
A	V	E	N	A	N	D	I	O	N	E	A	R	T
H	A	M	E	N	C	W	O	B	M	M	V	P	B
R	E	C	O	M	M	E	N	D	A	T	I	O	N

5 Complete each sentence with the best adverb. More than one answer may be possible.

badly	hardly	highly	perfectly
totally	widely		

1 'I'm afraid your work is so .... written that I refuse to mark it,' the teacher said.
2 The product was .... recommended by some friends of mine.
3 To be .... honest with you, no, I didn't enjoy the shopping trip.
4 Tom was .... amazed to find his cat asleep in the washing machine.
5 'It's .... necessary to take such a large bag when you go shopping,' she said.
6 The new restaurant was .... advertised in all the papers and on radio.
7 Professor Sims has always been a .... respected member of the faculty.
8 These types of machine are .... available in the shops.

6 Which word/phrase in each set doesn't collocate with *decision* or *choice*?

1 a *great / total / wise / unanimous* decision
2 a *popular / smooth / hard / snap* decision
3 to *make / have / offer / stop* a choice
4 a(n) *obvious / odd / soft / wide* choice
5 to be *spoilt for / given a/the / made a/the / left with no* choice

7 Complete these sentences with one of the collocations from exercise 6.

1 In the end, everyone agreed, making it a .... decision.
2 Dr Peters was given the Chair in Physics – he was the .... choice, as he had been acting Chair for the past two years.
3 When the rain came down, we had to make a .... decision – time wasn't on our side.
4 In the shop, we were .... the choice of either having a refund or a credit note.
5 Stella was .... choice in the shoe shop and didn't know which pair she liked most.

8 Complete the text with the appropriate form of one of these phrases to do with shopping.

a bargain	to cost a fortune	half price
to keep the receipt	a reasonable price	
a refund	to try something on	
to window shop		

During the holidays, I decided to do a bit of 1 .... As I walked through the mall, I could see that there were quite a few 2 .... to be had. Some things were 3 .... or less. The last pair of shoes I bought 4 .... , and so I really wanted something at a more 5 .... Suddenly, I saw a pair of trainers – they were just what I needed, so I asked the assistant if I could 6 .... They fitted perfectly, and I made up my mind immediately to get them. As the assistant was putting them in a bag for me, she told me to 7 .... , just in case I changed my mind and needed to get a 8 ....

Reading

1 Look at the words in the box. Put them in pairs with similar meanings.

EXAMPLE: *a colour – a pigment*

clear	~~a colour~~	a consideration	to create
to extract	genuine	an issue	to make	real
~~a pigment~~	to take out	transparent

2 Read the text below. Time yourself as you read.

⏲ about 700 words

A

There are no 'real' colours in nature – only the various wavelengths that make up light, which are absorbed and reflected by all the objects around us. The reflected wavelengths enter the eye, which, in turn, sends signals to
5 the brain: only then do we 'see' the impact of all these wavelengths on the eye. This white light contains the colours of the rainbow, which can be seen when the rays are separated by a glass prism. Each colour has its own wavelength: violet has the shortest, and red the longest.
10 When these colours are combined with nature's pigments – the chlorophyll in grass, for instance – millions of shades can be created. Painters have reproduced these using the powdered colours of natural or artificial pigments which are themselves only the colour of the light they reflect.

B

15 However, before we can adequately explore what colour means to the artist, we must ask what we mean by the word 'colour'. This may seem straightforward enough, but is my 'red' the same as your 'red'? Linguistic considerations are often central to an interpretation of
20 the historical use of colour in art. The Japanese *awo* can mean 'green', 'blue' or 'dark', depending on the context; Vietnamese also declines to distinguish green from blue. The indigenous Australians, the Aborigines, only have two colour terms – white and black – even though they
25 use other colours in their paintings. English uses 11 colour words – black, white, red, orange, yellow, green, blue, purple, pink, grey and brown – and thousands of other 'borrowed' names – apricot, avocado, gold, peach and so on.

C

30 Before the 19th century, when artists were deciding which colour paint to use, they generally had to use 'natural products', which is to say organic substances derived from animals and plants. The earliest cave paintings were made using red from iron oxides, black
35 from charcoal and white from chalk and ground bones. Later, Tyrian purple, the imperial colour of ancient Rome,

was extracted from a particular shellfish – just under half a kilo of royal purple dye required the crushing of four million molluscs. Cochineal red, discovered by the Aztecs, was made using the female cochineal beetle. 40

D

Interestingly, however, the blue pigment known as Egyptian frit or Egyptian blue, which has been identified in artefacts dating from around 2500 BC, is not a naturally occurring product. It was made by the ancient Egyptians who needed to first of all mix different compounds 45 together and then heat them. This resulted in the oldest synthetic pigment, a Bronze Age blue. This use of nature's materials reveals ancient Egypt as a civilisation with a genuine command of chemistry.

E

The cost and quality of the colours used were factors to be 50 born in mind by both artist and patron when a painting was commissioned. The dramatic red, made from a substance called cinnabar, used to paint wall panels in Pompeii, Italy, around 60 BC, was mined in Spain and was so expensive that a law was passed setting a ceiling 55 price. Another colour, ultramarine blue, was extracted from the lapis lazuli stone, which had to be quarried and shipped from Afghanistan. The expense of this meant that, in western art, ultramarine blue was reserved for paintings of very special or important people. 60

F

A new technique in the early 15th century expanded the range of colours that could be portrayed with oil paint. In this technique, the powdered pigment is mixed with a slow-drying oil – such as linseed or walnut – which absorbs oxygen from the air, forming a transparent skin 65 that locks the colour in. This meant that oil paint could be built up in layers and so only three or four pigments could be used to create over 20 different shades of, say, red. In the 19th century, the invention of collapsible tin paint-tubes to replace pigs' bladders made paint much 70 more portable.

G

So, where will artists get their colour inspiration from next? Perhaps more metallic or fluorescent colours will be used, or perhaps artists will use liquid crystals that change colour with temperature or that offer an 75 iridescent rainbow all at once. One thing is certain: technology will always open new doors for artists.

3 Which paragraph contains the following information? You may use any letter more than once.
···⟩ TF7

1 why there was a need for state intervention
2 an account of how humans perceive colour
3 the reason why the use of a colour was limited
4 details of the first known production of an artificial colour
5 a reference to different living organisms used in the production of colours
6 the part played by two important technical developments
7 different ways of putting the idea of colour into words
8 the way in which a colour could be made lighter or darker
9 an example of languages using the same word for more than one colour
10 where raw materials had to be dug out of the ground

Grammar

-ing forms and infinitives

G ···⟩ STUDENT'S BOOK pages 141 and 142

4 Correct these errors which IELTS candidates have made.

1 I have experience to design colour schemes for offices.
2 Can I suggest to go to see the science museum?
3 The interior of the car is designed for improving driving.
4 Leila learned using watercolour paints at college.
5 Let Pablo going into the room first.
6 He will be under pressure to meet deadlines and completing tasks and coursework.
7 You must to go and see the new colours at the fashion show.
8 In conclusion, to study abroad has fewer advantages than in this country.
9 To let everyone to know where the talk will be held, there'll be a map.
10 She intends to going away after term ends.
11 Pete can't remember to get into the car and to drive to the station.
12 We prevented to him draw on the walls.
13 A lot of time was spent to teach them to write.
14 Try to walk rather than to drive everywhere if you want to lose weight.
15 It was years ago, but I'll never forget to see Venice for the first time.
16 You'd better ringing up your tutor to tell him you'll be late.
17 Elisa's interested to do fashion design next term.
18 Remember posting that letter on your way to work.
19 Children often dream to be football stars.
20 You need giving up staying up late watching TV.

Vocabulary

5 Complete the definitions with the words in the box.

appreciative   cautious   competent
honest   impatient   impulsive
independent   sensitive

1 A(n) .... person is one who quickly gets annoyed if they have to wait for someone.
2 A(n) .... person is helpful and kind and knows what other people need.
3 A(n) .... person always writes a note to thank someone who gives them a present.
4 A(n) .... person always does things well.
5 A(n) .... person is not easily influenced by other people.
6 A(n) .... person avoids taking risks.
7 A(n) .... person can always be trusted.
8 A(n) .... person does things without planning or considering what might happen.

15 Social interaction

Vocabulary

1 These words come from the reading passage and exercise 3 in 15.1 of the Student's Book. Using the clues, write the words in the grid and find the secret word.

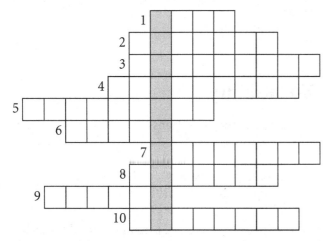

1 someone who invites another person to their home
2 complicated
3 crucial
4 dear, costing a great deal
5 food bought from shops and markets
6 someone invited to another person's home
7 sufficient, enough for a particular purpose
8 to watch carefully, to notice
9 informal
10 someone who lives in a particular place

Secret word: friendly and welcoming to people invited to one's home ....

Grammar

Must and *can't*

G ···⟩ STUDENT'S BOOK page 142

2 The *Cambridge Learner Corpus* shows that many IELTS candidates find modal verbs difficult. Read these sentences and correct any mistakes in the phrases in **bold**. Some of them are correct.

1 Young people like to use the telephone and watch TV at night. If their parents want to sleep, the noise **must make** them unhappy.

2 My brother felt shy when my aunt and uncle visited us. We concluded that he **must be spent** too much time watching television. *have* *must*

3 The leak is low, near to the floor, so it **should be related** to the pipes of the shower behind it. *must*

4 I invited Abdul to come tomorrow, so that **mustn't be** him now. *can't*

5 Many people take part in dangerous sports, so there **must be** some who have accidents.

6 You **must haven't attend** a Chinese wedding before, as you are surprised by this one. *can't have*

7 I believe that retirement at 60 or 65 is a good idea. One reason is that people **should be** tired at that age. *must*

8 This food contains so much sugar that it **not can be** healthy.

9 I keep seeing Deirdre in town, so she **mustn't be working** in France any more. *can't*

Reading

3 Read the passage on the next page. Which paragraph mentions the following information? You may use any letter more than once. ···⟩ TF7

1 a list of motives for developing social relationships C
2 an example of people wishing to learn about a future experience from others E
3 various forms that social activities can take A
4 how social relationships can be used to evaluate one's own feelings D/E
5 a classification of occasions when people prefer to be alone or with other people F
6 a comparison between the behaviour of adults and children E
7 an outline of stages in the development of social relationships B
8 how an investigation was carried out F
9 why children behave as they do B
10 a reason for a claim concerning the role of social relationships in daily life A (?)

⏱ about 450 words

Social relationships

A Imagine for a minute what life would be like without social relationships: not swapping news with your family at the end of the day, not gossiping with your friends about the party you went to last night, not chatting with colleagues at the coffee machine, not having any close relationship involving mutual support and caring. Imagining this kind of life is so difficult as to be almost impossible, which neatly illustrates the importance of social relationships in our lives. `10`

B From the earliest age, humans want to belong to their world and to feel a sense of connectedness with it. This need for belonging can be observed as the motivation for infants in their earliest interactions with others. From the moment of birth, babies seek `15` to establish an enduring social relationship with their main carer, extending their circle of relationships outwards as skills and circumstances allow. Later, as their social skills improve, children modify their behaviour to others in order to fit in with other `20` people and gain a sense of belonging.

C Wanting to belong is thought to be a basic need, which makes us set up, keep and – when necessary – repair good social relations with others. It has been suggested that we create social relations for `25` four main reasons: to enable us to compare ourselves with others, thereby reducing uncertainty; to obtain the reward of stimulating company; to be valued; and to gain emotional support.

D Social comparison allows participants to measure `30` their own uncertainty against that of other people and decide, for instance, whether their fear is justified. It can thus be a strategy for reducing anxiety.

E Relationships can also be used for information seeking. Just as young children refer to their parents `35` for information in new or ambiguous situations, adults will also seek out someone with more information when in difficulty. Hospital patients facing an operation the next day generally prefer to spend the night with others who have already had `40` the operation and can provide information about the potential danger, rather than with someone who is about to undergo the same operation.

F In one piece of research, people were asked to specify the conditions under which they would like `45` to be with others. The researcher found that people preferred the company of others in pleasant conditions, such as enjoying a concert, when feeling happy or in the work environment. Company was also preferred in threatening conditions, such as `50` when in danger or feeling afraid. In unpleasant conditions, such as when feeling tense or having just failed a test, people preferred to be alone, as they did in conditions requiring them to concentrate, such as solving a complicated problem `55` or making a decision.

4 After each adjective there are five nouns. Four of them often collocate with the adjective. Cross through the one that does NOT normally collocate. It will help if you find the adjectives in the passage.

EXAMPLE: mutual *advantage / benefit / respect / ~~situation~~ / support*

1 (a) complicated *history / problem / relationship / rules / value*
2 (an) emotional *appeal / motivation / relationship / response / support*
3 (a) social *conditions / group / interaction / operation / skills*
4 (a) stimulating *approach / belonging / company / discussion / effect*
5 (a) potential *consequences / customer / difficulty / danger / hospital*
6 (a) threatening *behaviour / conditions / environment / need / situation*

Check your answers before you go on to exercise 5.

5 Choose one of the four nouns from the appropriate set in exercise 4 to complete these sentences. Check both the meaning and the grammar.

EXAMPLE: Almost everyone participates in social ....*interaction*..... at home and at work.

1 As babies develop, they manage to work out and learn the complicated .... of the language they hear around them.
2 Any relationship between two people can be damaged by the threatening .... of one participant.
3 If the two participants in a relationship lack mutual .... , the relationship is unlikely to be long-lasting.
4 As children become more skilful, they learn to identify, and to some extent avoid, the potential .... of their actions.
5 The presentation was followed by a stimulating .... of the role of emotions in social relationships.
6 The speaker made an emotional .... for conflict to be resolved by peaceful means.
7 Social .... is important for children, as it helps them to learn how to behave.

Books, writing and signs

Reading

1 Read this book review, and complete the table below. Choose NO MORE THAN TWO WORDS from the passage for each answer.
···▸ TF3 (Completing a table is very similar to completing notes.)

⏱ about 340 words

Insights into the alphabet

In his book *Letter Perfect* (originally published under the title *Language Visible*), David Sacks proves that an area of language that we generally overlook is much more interesting than we might imagine: as the 26 building
5 blocks of our written language, the letters of our alphabet have an enormous impact on our lives. Serious linguists might find this book frustrating, but Sacks's target audience seems to be casual linguists, and they will love it. He sets out to educate and entertain us by exploring
10 both the history and the modern significance of each letter of the alphabet in turn.

Sacks is the author of *Encyclopaedia of the Ancient Greek World* and numerous articles on cultural topics, including 26 on the alphabet that he wrote for a
15 Canadian newspaper. These were so popular that he was encouraged to develop them into this book, which is full of fascinating information. He writes about how the Roman, Cyrillic, Arabic, Greek and Hebrew alphabets have descended from a common ancestor which was

created around 4,000 years ago. We learn why in English 20 the letter C is sometimes pronounced like S and sometimes like K, why Americans say *zee* for Z while the British prefer *zed*, and why Q is always followed by U. His comments on the letters in the present day cover everything from B-movies, through the character M of 25 James Bond films, to the Thomas Pynchon novel *V*.

The downside of the one-chapter-per-letter structure, however, is that it leads to considerable repetition: for instance, several chapters tell us about the origins of the Roman alphabet. Another drawback of the book is that 30 the dual focus on history and modern culture doesn't quite work. When he writes about the past, it is scholarly but can appear uninteresting, while what he says about the present sometimes seems unscholarly.

Many people will find plenty to interest them in this 35 book, though it's probably better to dip into it at random, rather than read it from cover to cover. It's a book that's sure to give plenty of pleasure.

Outline of book review	
Introduction	
Title	1 ....
Author	2 ....
Category	3 ....
Subject area	*alphabet*
Intended readers	4 ....
Overview	
Author's purpose	*to educate and entertain*
Main topics	*the 5 .... and current 6 .... of every letter*
Analysis and evaluation • Qualifications to write about subject • Strengths • Weaknesses	• *has written an encyclopaedia and many 7 ....* • *contains plenty of interesting 8 ....* • *too much 9 .... between chapters* • *sections about the past can seem 10 ....* • *sections about the present can seem 11 ....*
Conclusion Overall response	*Enjoyable, especially if you don't read it from 12 .... to ....*

Vocabulary

2 The words in the box are related to ones in the reading passage in 16.1 of the Student's Book. Use them in the correct form to complete the sentences below. A brief definition is given in italics.

abstract	alphabetical	combine
communicative	evolve	indicate
modify	predecessor	regular
representational	significant	unrelated

1 English spelling has .... over a period of about 1,300 years. (*develop*)
2 One category of Egyptian hieroglyphs .... what type of meaning a word has. (*show*)
3 The vast majority of Chinese characters are very ...., and so it is impossible to guess their meanings. (*non realistic*)
4 When the Latin alphabet was adopted for Turkish in 1928, it was partially .... so that all the sounds of the language could be represented. (*adapt*)
5 Letters are used for the sounds of a language that are .... for distinguishing between words, for example, *fed* and *red*. (*important*)
6 Finnish spelling is much more .... than English. (*consistent*)
7 The sign 'No dogs allowed' consists of a fairly .... image of a dog, with a diagonal red line that symbolises prohibition. (*pictorial*)
8 The Egyptian hieroglyphic system was a far more effective means of communication than its .... (*the one that it replaced*)

3 Write these words under the verb that they are more likely to follow.

a book	a (book) review	a dissertation
an email	an essay	an experiment
an investigation	a letter	a report
research	a survey	a threat	a thesis

to write	to carry out
a book	

4 Complete these sentences with words from exercise 3. In some cases, more than one answer is possible.

1 The museum asked the police to carry out a detailed .... into the disappearance of some valuable books.
2 A telephone .... of 1,000 people showed considerable support for the idea of simplifying spelling.
3 When Jane wrote up the results of her ...., she realised that some of her claims were contradictory.
4 I found that another student had chosen the same research topic for her ...., so I had to change my focus.
5 The college has just issued its annual ...., which shows a major investment in equipment for the library.
6 Dr Barton was delighted to read a favourable .... of his new book in a leading journal.

Grammar

Non-finite clauses

G ⋯⋗ STUDENT'S BOOK page 142

5 Rewrite each pair of sentences as one sentence, using one of the words in the box and a non-finite verb. This will help you to write in an academic style.

after	before	by	despite	for	while

EXAMPLE: Sacks sets out to educate and entertain us. His method is to explore both the history and the modern significance of each letter.

Sacks sets out to educate and entertain us, by exploring both the history and the modern significance of each letter.

1 I recommend that you read this book. Then you should write your assignment about the Roman alphabet.
2 I only managed to finish the book before the deadline. I read it without stopping.
3 Writing a book review is a useful tool. It helps you to think carefully about what you have read.
4 I enjoyed reading *Letter Perfect*. This was even though I found it repetitive in places.
5 I read *Letter Perfect*. I then understood much more about the alphabet.
6 Many readers will be irritated by some parts of the book. At the same time, they will enjoy other parts.
7 They are related. However the Latin and Arabic alphabets are very different from each other.

The body clock

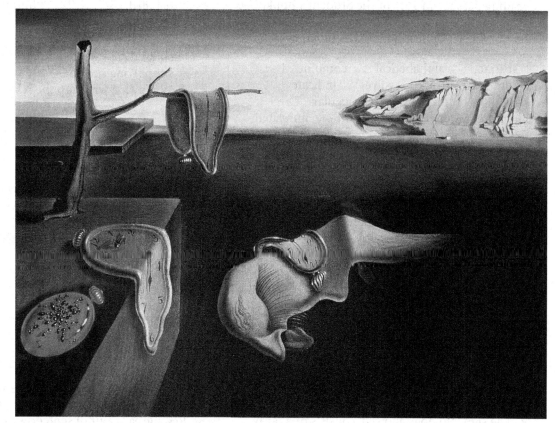

Vocabulary

1 Match the sentences in column A with the *time* collocations in column B.

A	B
1 That film I saw was terrible.	**a** I wasted my time going to see it.
2 I'd better go or I'll be late.	**b** I spend too much time watching TV.
3 I won't rush.	**c** I pass the time walking and reading.
4 I have nothing to do until the shift ends.	**d** I don't have the time.
5 It's a great place to relax.	**e** I'll take my time.
6 I'm not going to do an evening class.	**f** I'll kill time reading a magazine.
7 I waste most of my evenings.	**g** I've run out of time – lunch is over.

2 Complete the health-related sentences below using the verbs in the box in the appropriate form.

catch	come down with	come out in	feel (×2)	get over	have (×2)
lose (×2)	make (×2)				

1 I .... sick, so I'm not going into work today.
2 I really can't eat anything – I .... (completely) my appetite.
3 Luisa .... a bad cold last week and had to have a couple of days off.
4 Come back to work when you .... a bit better.
5 When Anna had measles, she .... spots all over her body.
6 Marco carried on with the job, even though he .... a terrible headache.
7 Our manager .... a full recovery from his operation last month.
8 The doctor asked Rory if he .... a temperature.
9 It only takes a few days .... a cold and return to normal.
10 When Paula .... her voice, she had to suck lozenges all day.
11 The factory was closed, as half the workers .... flu.
12 Don't eat too many biscuits – you'll .... yourself ill.

3 Complete the sentence with an appropriate form of *make* or *do*.

EXAMPLE: 'What do you ...*do*... for a living?' 'I ...*do*... shift work at the local factory.'

1 Pete .... a course at the local college at the moment.
2 I think you .... a mistake working nights.
3 We should .... a complaint about the number of hours we work.
4 My boss .... a fortune from his tyre factory.
5 My brother's so lazy – he .... (never) a day's work in his life.
6 You need to have a hot drink – it .... you good and .... you feel better.
7 We'll all have to .... without our tea breaks in future.
8 The manager .... his best to be fair about the night shift this month.
9 We're not allowed to .... phone calls from work.
10 .... me a favour, will you? Don't .... a noise when you go to bed.
11 Marcia .... a huge fuss when she found her hours had been changed.
12 'What time .... (you) it?' 'Ten past three.'

4 These words are all taken from 17.1 of the Student's Book. Complete the table, where possible, with the other forms of the words given. Use an English-English dictionary to help you.

Noun (abstract)	Adjective	Verb	Noun (person)
1	2	regulate	3
4	psychological		5
6	7	8	consultant
evolution	9	10	11
12	13	vary	
14	communicative	15	16
17	18	manage	19
20	21	destroy	22
23	natural		24
information	25	26	27
length	28	29	
30	31	32	humans

Grammar

Modals: obligation, lack of obligation and prohibition

G ⋯⋮ STUDENT'S BOOK page 142

5 Underline the correct modal verb.

EXAMPLE: We *must* / *have to* walk to work now the buses are on strike.

1 You *must* / *have to* visit us when you're next in Sydney.
2 Paul, you *mustn't* / *don't have to* touch that machinery – it's dangerous!
3 You *mustn't* / *don't have to* make a coffee for me – I've just had one.
4 Jo, you *don't have to* / *mustn't* rush to work this morning – it's Saturday.
5 The manager says we *have to* / *mustn't* be late on Tuesday.
6 Nurses *have to* / *mustn't* wear a uniform.
7 Attention! Workers *must* / *have to* wear a hard hat on this site at all times.
8 When I broke my leg, I *didn't have to* / *had to* walk with sticks, which was very uncomfortable.

6 Correct these errors made by IELTS candidates (some include *need*).

1 You must to check whether the electricity is switched off before you touch the plug.
2 Everyone need have electricity today.
3 People must working at least eight hours a day to qualify as full-time workers.
4 We hasn't need of any products to help us sleep.
5 We not have to take a nap this afternoon as we're too busy.
6 How much sleep you need must depends on how tired you are.
7 They have not to rest now.
8 You don't must drive when you're tired.

Reading

1 **Skim the text and answer these questions.**

1 Where would you find an article like this?
2 What is the writer's purpose in writing this article?
3 Is the writer's impression of Antarctica favourable or unfavourable?

⏱ about 575 words

A TRIP TO THE END OF THE WORLD

The pilot's reassuring voice came over the public address system as our Qantas 747 went down the runway at Sydney Airport in Australia: 'We'll be taking off in a southerly direction.' Watch check: 8.20 a.m. Our day trip had begun. We were going to Antarctica. For the first four hours – most of which was a straight line across the ocean – we could have been anywhere, but what makes the outbound journey memorable is the opportunity to study the science and history of the seventh continent as presented by those who have lived and worked there.

There were four specialists on this particular trip: Pat Quilty, geologist and retired chief of the Australian Antarctic programme; Polar Medal-winner Syd Kirkby, who has surveyed more Antarctic territory than any other polar explorer; Di Patterson, the first woman appointed to run an Antarctic research station; and Warren Papworth, who knows more about emperor penguins than the penguins themselves. Instead of in-flight movies, we were entertained, awed and painlessly educated about Antarctica.

Until roughly 160 million years ago, Antarctica was part of the ancient continent of Gondwanaland, before Gondwanaland split up into the continents we know today. A few minutes before noon, the pilot, Captain Dennis, urged us all to take out the compasses we'd been asked to bring. As I placed mine on my knee, the needle moved away from north-south and began to spin wildly. We were passing directly over the South Magnetic Pole. Unlike the geographic pole, it moves about 6km a year.

As I peered through my window at the Southern Ocean below, the outermost ice floes were visible directly beneath the wing, resembling pieces of a vast natural jigsaw. Then came Dumont d'Urville, a base on Antarctica. We continued east along the coast before turning south over the Ross Ice Shelf.

By the end of these middle four hours of the journey, we had seen ice-cliffs, powder ice, amazing blue ice (even the scientists don't know what makes it so), many varieties of glacier and, last but not least, magnificent rivers of ice sliding into the sea. All this grandeur largely offset any disappointment at not glimpsing the penguins which Antarctica is famous for, let alone a colony. The reason was sound enough: to fly low enough to see the penguins clearly would seriously disturb them.

We passed the Transantarctic mountains, which Captain Dennis said were 'one of the loveliest mountain ranges on the surface of the Earth'. But for me, the highlight of this unforgettable day trip was Mount Minto, which soars more than 4,000m above the Ross Ice Shelf.

All too soon, it was time to bank around in a half-circle and begin the trip back to Sydney and civilisation. This is one trip that can certainly be recommended to those people who want to do something a bit different. From November to February, the 'season' for doing Antarctica, the weather is remarkably consistent. The outside air temperature is around freezing, but very sunny. Because you won't be putting down anywhere, the journey is classed as a domestic flight, so – sad to say – you won't get an Antarctic stamp in your passport, something which you don't need to carry on this trip. But, by way of compensation, you will receive a commemorative certificate declaring that you have crossed the Antarctic continent, 'thereby joining the exclusive group of travellers who have achieved this feat'.

2 Complete this summary. Choose NO MORE THAN THREE WORDS AND/OR A NUMBER from the passage for each answer. Remember, the words must be in the passage. ⋯⫶ TF5

The trip to Antarctica started from **1** .... Airport at 8.20 in the morning. During the first part of the trip, the writer was given some background information on the continent by **2** .... who were accompanying the flight. They explained that Antarctica as we know it had only existed for the last **3** .... Before that, it had been part of Gondwanaland.

The writer discovered that a compass needle was no longer aligned **4** .... when the plane was above the South Magnetic Pole – a pole which changes position by around **5** .... a year. Besides the pole, the writer flew over the **6** .... at Dumont d'Urville. The writer was particularly impressed by the mysterious **7** .... , but was saddened not to have seen any **8** .... However, he understood why this was not possible. What made the trip **9** .... for the writer was seeing Mount Minto, which is 4,000m high.

Anyone can take this trip, which takes place from **10** .... The plane doesn't land, so there is no need for a **11** .... However, a **12** .... is given out to all participants.

Vocabulary

3 Find the ten 'travel' words from Unit 18 in the Student's Book in this wordsearch. (↓ → ↘)

D	B	A	C	K	P	A	C	K	E	R	A
T	E	R	E	Q	B	U	K	G	D	S	B
R	I	S	I	H	N	O	M	X	C	B	R
A	Z	C	T	X	O	N	O	B	R	C	O
V	R	E	I	I	U	T	T	K	U	M	A
E	S	D	V	B	N	L	E	A	I	W	D
L	T	E	C	B	R	A	U	L	S	E	D
L	T	O	U	R	I	S	T	K	E	F	G
E	O	E	R	U	Q	E	R	I	N	V	C
R	W	G	F	K	U	O	E	H	O	D	H
E	S	I	G	H	T	S	E	E	I	N	G
T	R	A	V	E	L	A	G	E	N	T	C

4 Put these words into the correct column of the table below.

cabin caravan cash exchange rate malaria pills notes self-catering apartment sunscreen tent travel-sickness pills traveller's cheques vaccination

Accommodation	Health	Money

Grammar

Phrasal verbs

G ⋯⫶ STUDENT'S BOOK page 143

5 Complete these sentences using the phrasal verbs in brackets and include a suitable noun, pronoun or verb.

EXAMPLES:
The hotel *takes on extra staff* every July and August when it is fully booked and more help is needed. (take on)
Your expenses on this trip were quite high – you should try to *keep them down* in future. (keep down)

1 The flight is overbooked – can anyone .... to this problem? (come up with)
2 Long-haul flights are awful – I find I can no longer .... (put up with)
3 It was hard to understand what the notice said, but in the end they succeeded in .... (make out)
4 My uncle started a travel agency last year – he .... with the help of a bank loan. (set up)
5 We no longer have our hotel – a large American hotel chain .... in June. (take over)
6 Thank you for your letter – I .... you at the travel conference next month. (look forward to)

Reading

⏱ about 575 words

HOW HELICOPTERS WORK

If you have ever flown in a helicopter, you know that it is an exciting experience. Helicopters can fly almost anywhere, because they are the most versatile flying machines in existence today. While virtually all planes can only fly forward, a helicopter is also able to fly backward and sideways. The main characteristic of a helicopter, of course, is that it can hover over one point, and simultaneously either stay motionless in the air, or rotate on its axis, giving the pilot a panoramic view of the ground below. A car or a plane, on the other hand, can only change direction if it is moving.

A helicopter can do a number of interesting tricks, such as rotating through 360 degrees while it travels down a straight line relative to the ground. A helicopter that is flying forward can also stop in mid-air and begin hovering very quickly. Maneuvers like these are impossible in a plane, which must fly forward at all times for its wings to provide lift.

The extra freedom that helicopters offer is what makes them so exciting, but it also makes them complex.

- -

The helicopter is controlled from the cockpit, the small area at the front where the pilot sits and looks out. The controls need to be within reach of the pilot's hands—and feet, as they include pedals.

The word *helicopter* is Greek in origin. *Heliko*—from *helix*—means a spiral, and *pteron* means a wing. To make it possible for the machine to fly upward, the wings have to be in motion, pushing air downward. It is this downward movement which creates the lift that raises the helicopter.

The easiest way to keep wings in continuous motion is to rotate them. This can be done by mounting two or more wings on a drive shaft and spinning the shaft, much like the blades on a ceiling fan. The rotating wings of a helicopter are generally narrow and thin because they must spin so quickly. The helicopter's rotating wing assembly is normally called the main rotor. If this is at a slight angle and the shaft spins, the wings start to push the air down and raise the helicopter. The main rotor is the most important part of the vehicle. As well as lifting it, it allows the helicopter to move laterally, make turns, and change altitude.

In order to spin the shaft with enough force to lift a human being and the helicopter, you need an engine. The engine's drive shaft is connected to the main rotor shaft. This arrangement works really well until the vehicle leaves the ground. At that moment, there is nothing to keep the engine (and therefore the body of the vehicle) from spinning in the opposite direction to the main rotor.

To keep the body from spinning, you need to apply a force to it. This is usually done by attaching another set of rotating wings to the tail boom, which is the section at the back of the helicopter, projecting from the main body. These wings are known as the tail rotor. The tail rotor pushes the air in a sideways direction, counteracting the engine's desire to spin the body, so this keeps the body of the helicopter from spinning.

The proper technique to land a helicopter is to touch down evenly with both landing skids touching the ground at all points at the same time. Otherwise there is a risk of severe vibration that can cause serious damage and possibly destroy the helicopter.

1 The article on page 40 is an American text about helicopters. Read it as far as the dotted line and complete the summary below. Choose NO MORE THAN ONE WORD from the passage for each answer. ⋯⫶ TF5

What makes helicopters so exciting

There is hardly any limit to where helicopters can fly, because they are more **1** .... than planes. Unlike planes, helicopters can fly both **2** .... and **3** .... In addition, they can **4** .... in one position and **5** .... at the same time, giving the pilot a view in any direction. Most planes can only gain **6** .... by flying forward.

2 Read the rest of the article and label the diagram below. Choose NO MORE THAN TWO WORDS from the passage for each answer. ⋯⫶ TF10

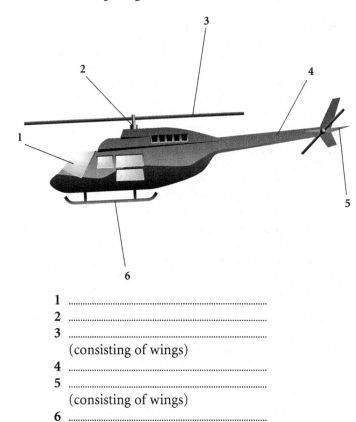

1 ....
2 ....
3 ....
(consisting of wings)
4 ....
5 ....
(consisting of wings)
6 ....

Grammar

Unreal present and future

G ⋯⫶ STUDENT'S BOOK page 143

3 Correct the mistakes in these sentences, which were written by IELTS candidates. One sentence is correct.

1 I wish creative artists don't do this.
2 I'd rather we drive in my car.
3 I think it is time we should discuss this problem.
4 I wish you should give me half my pay before the weekend, but I don't suppose you will.
5 Some children have paid jobs, but many people would rather they didn't.
6 It is about time students, families and society all realise there is a problem and recognise their own responsibilities!
7 It is high time the government pay women who stay at home to look after their children.

Vocabulary

4 Complete the passage below using words from the box. Notice how the passive is used in this fairly formal description of the light rail system; this is typical of Task 1 of the Academic Writing Module.

accessible	capacity	congestion
conventional	damage	ease	elevated
extension	linked	produce	reliable
seats		

*Light*rail

Light rail is an attractive way of moving large numbers of passengers along busy routes, and town planners are increasingly turning to it to **1** .... the problems of urban traffic **2** ....

A typical two-car unit **3** .... 64 passengers, and with space for many more standing at peak times, they have a far greater **4** .... than a typical bus. Units can also be **5** .... to form longer trains. The vehicles are **6** .... to all, including parents with small children and the elderly or mobility-impaired. In some computer-controlled systems, the train is driverless.

Tracks are set beside or in the middle of streets or on **7** .... bridge sections. Compared with **8** .... trains, there can be more frequent stops. With segregated tracks, there are no traffic jams, and the service is safe and **9** .... Light rail is one of the most environmentally friendly forms of transport. There are no fumes to **10** .... the environment, and vehicles are quiet.

Moving abroad

Reading

This passage comes from a booklet called *Welcome to Australia!*, published by the Australian Government for people who have just moved to the country. It is similar to the passages found in Section 1 of the General Training Reading Module, while the tasks below are found in both Reading Modules.

⏱ about 425 words

Welcome to Australia!

Apply for a Tax File Number
Everyone who receives any income in Australia needs a Tax File Number. Income includes wages or salary from a job, money earned from investments, and government payments.

Register with Medicare
The Australian Government provides help with medical expenses through a scheme called Medicare. You may be eligible to join Medicare and gain immediate access to health-care services and programs such as free public hospital care, help with the cost of out-of-hospital care and subsidised medicines.

To register with Medicare, you should wait approximately ten working days after your arrival in Australia and then go to a Medicare office, listed in the telephone book, with your passport or travel documents. If you need to see a doctor urgently, you can register with Medicare without waiting ten days.

Medicare has a *Welcome Kit* which is translated into 16 different languages. It explains Medicare and other government health services and the eligibility requirements for benefits and payments. This booklet is available from Medicare offices or you can read it on the Internet.

Open a bank account
People in Australia usually keep their money in a bank, building society or credit union. It is advisable to open a bank account within six weeks of your arrival, as during this time you usually need only your passport as identification. After six weeks, you will need additional identification to open an account.

Register with Centrelink
Newly arrived residents can register with the government agency called Centrelink to get help with looking for work, having overseas skills recognised, and accessing relevant courses. Centrelink also has an application form for Tax File Numbers and can assist you to lodge your application with the Tax Office, so that access to any payments is not delayed.

Register for English classes
English language courses for new arrivals in Australia are provided under the Adult Migrant English Program. As a new resident, you may be entitled to receive free English language tuition of up to 510 hours.

Get a driver's licence
If you are a permanent resident visa holder and have a current driver's licence from another country, in English or with an official translation, you are allowed to drive for your first three months after arrival. After that, if you want to drive, you will need to have the appropriate Australian driver's licence. To get one, you usually need to pass a knowledge test, a practical test, and an eyesight test. Licences from some overseas countries do not require a practical test.

1 Read the passage. Do the statements on page 43 agree with the information given in the passage? ⋯⟩ TF1

Write

TRUE	*if the statement agrees with the information*
FALSE	*if the statement contradicts the information*
NOT GIVEN	*if there is no information on this*

1 A Tax File Number is only required by people who are working.
2 All health-care services are free for people registered with Medicare.
3 In certain cases, it is possible to register with Medicare less than ten days after arriving in Australia.
4 There is a charge for Welcome Kit booklets obtained from Medicare offices.
5 Banks are the most commonly used form of financial institution.
6 If you open a bank account in your first six weeks in Australia, you will probably need fewer documents than later on.
7 Centrelink can help you to get your qualifications accepted officially.
8 Centrelink can lend money to new arrivals if necessary.
9 English language lessons are offered at no cost to all new residents who require them.
10 Whether or not you need to take an Australian practical test for a driver's licence depends on which country you come from.

2 **Complete the sentences below with words taken from the passage. Write NO MORE THAN THREE WORDS AND/OR A NUMBER for each answer.** ⋯⟩ TF3

1 The address of the nearest Medicare office can be found in a ....
2 You can work out from the Medicare *Welcome Kit* whether or not you are entitled to .... from the government.
3 Centrelink can help you with your .... for payments from the Tax Office.
4 The Adult Migrant English Program offers a maximum of .... of English lessons.
5 All foreign driver's licences can be used for .... without taking any part of the Australian driving test.
6 Holders of all foreign driver's licences are required to pass the .... and .... tests.

Vocabulary

3 The sentences below are about the earliest Inuit and European settlers in Greenland. Most of them contain one of the phrasal verbs from 20.2 in the Student's Book. ⋯⟩ TF3

Complete each sentence (1–8) with the best ending (a–i) below. There is one ending that you will not need to use.

1 The earliest Inuit settlers (formerly known as Eskimos) had to put up with
2 In such difficult conditions, they had to work at
3 When the climate turned colder, they dealt with
4 Most of the early European settlers had been brought up
5 Many of them had set off
6 Settlers from Iceland were looking forward to
7 Unlike Iceland, however, Greenland failed to live up to
8 The Icelanders arrived in a land that turned out

a a green, fertile island.
b the change by moving south.
c to be very cold and largely covered by glaciers.
d cold weather and very little food.
e making life in Greenland bearable.
f from Iceland to avoid conflicts there.
g during a voyage across the North Atlantic.
h its name.
i in Iceland or Norway.

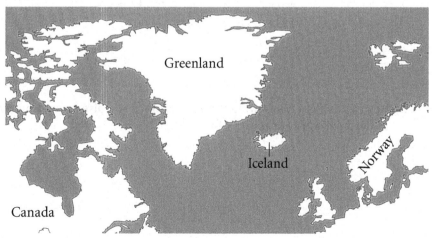

General Training Writing Task 1

1 Complete this advice on writing letters by circling the best option in italics.

  1 You *must / shouldn't* include an address.
  2 You can write *under / just over* 150 words.
  3 It is *acceptable / unacceptable* to begin 'Dear Mr Manager'.
  4 You *should / don't need to* check your grammar and spelling.
  5 You *don't have to / should* split your letter into paragraphs.
  6 You *can / shouldn't* end a formal letter with 'Yours faithfully'.
  7 A *good / inappropriate* way to end a formal letter is with 'I look forward to hearing from you in the near future'.
  8 *Make sure you use / Don't worry about using* appropriate language.

2 The letter below is based on an example from the *Cambridge Learner's Corpus*. It contains some errors that an IELTS candidate has made.

  a Read through the letter and decide whether it is successful in following the advice above. Ignore the numbers for the moment.

Hampstead, London

Dear **1** <u>Mr Councillor</u>, I am writing to **2** <u>complaint</u> about two large dogs that run in **3** <u>park</u> every evening. The owner of **4** <u>some</u> dogs, a young man, releases them to play in **5** <u>a</u> park, but I think it is **6** <u>so</u> dangerous **7** <u>to</u> people and animals to share this park. This has been happening **8** <u>since two weeks ago</u>, and I have watched the dogs and the owner from my house. My house is a large detached house in Bedford Drive, and I have lived there for twenty years. The most dangerous thing is that the dogs bark very loudly and **9** <u>running</u> towards people so that they **10** <u>afraid</u> them, especially small **11** <u>kids</u>. In fact, some people, including myself, **12** <u>attempt</u> to talk with the **13** <u>dog's</u> owner, but he seems to ignore what we say. As a **14** <u>mum</u> **15** <u>whose</u> two children, I am naturally worried about their safety. I am sending this letter **16** <u>because</u> a representative of a concerned group of park users. The owner needs to be told to keep his dogs on a leash so that people don't feel **17** <u>scary</u>. I am **18** <u>look</u> forward to **19** <u>hear</u> from you. **20** <u>Best wishes,</u>

(187 words)

  b Rewrite the letter, following the advice above and also correcting the underlined words or phrases for 1–20.

3 a Read this General Training Module Task 1 and underline the key words and phrases.

> *You want to sell your bicycle. You think a friend of yours might like to buy it from you.*
>
> *Write a letter to your friend. In your letter*
> - *explain why you are selling*
> - *describe the bicycle*
> - *suggest a date when your friend can come and see the bicycle.*
>
> Write at least 150 words.

b The sample letter below has eight spaces. Complete it by putting a word or phrase from the box in each space.

> asking   brand new   come round
> fine   give you   include   looked at
> make   new   serviced   ship
> take   type   very good condition
> visit   wondering

Dear Alex,

As you know, I'll be going home at the end of term and I've decided that I need to sell my bicycle — it would cost me too much to **1** .... it home to Manila. I was **2** .... if you might be interested in buying it.

It's a mountain bike, four years old now, and it was **3** .... when I bought it. Its green and black with a silver stripe. I have looked after it very well, having it **4** .... every year. The tyres are in **5** .... , and I am happy to **6** .... lights and a cycling helmet in the price. It's a Raleigh bicycle — a very good **7** .... — and I would like to sell it for around £40.

Why don't you **8** .... and have a look sometime? What about next Saturday morning when we don't have lectures?

Give me a ring and let me know.

Best wishes
Alicia

(154 words)

c Underline (an) example(s) of the following in the letter.

1 an explanation
2 a description
3 a suggestion

4 Correct the 12 spelling mistakes in this paragraph.

I'm writting to ask you for a six-month period of leave. I'm very much interested in computers, but unfortunaty I have poor computer skils. Last week, I saw an advertisment for a computer course on the TV. Though the unvirsity is in a diferent province, it is very famous, and the enrolment fee is not expensiv. So I want to attend the course. There I can aquire a lot of knowlege about computers and softwear. The course begins the day after tomorow. When I finnish the course, I will return to my job.

5 Match the purposes (1–6) with the letter extracts (a–f).

1 Suggesting
2 Complaining
3 Inviting
4 Explaining
5 Thanking
6 Apologising

a ... and if you are able to come on Monday evening, you will be very welcome.
b This really can't go on. I am not able to get any sleep at all.
c The reason I have not been able to hand in my work is that ...
d It was really very kind of you ...
e I think it would be a very good idea if we ...
f I promise this will not happen again and am very embarrassed that you had to complain in this way.

6 Do this Task 1.

> *An English-speaking friend is coming to study at your college next year and has written asking for information and advice.*
>
> *Write a letter to your friend. In your letter*
> - *give advice about accommodation in the town*
> - *describe the best thing about the college*
> - *offer to show your friend around the college.*
>
> Write at least 150 words.
>
> You do **NOT** need to write any addresses.
>
> Begin your letter as follows:
>
> **Dear ...**

Writing workout 2: Structuring an essay

General Training and Academic Writing Task 2

1 Look at this Task 2 and think about how you might answer it.

> **Below are five popular jobs. State which three you consider to be the most important to society today.**
>
> **doctor**
> **teacher**
> **engineer**
> **computer programmer**
> **journalist**
>
> Give reasons for your answer and include any relevant examples from your own knowledge or experience.
>
> Write at least 250 words.

2 Read the following two essays. Which one do you think would achieve higher marks? Think about:

1 how well the question is answered
2 how the essay is organised
3 if there are relevant examples of personal experience/knowledge
4 the range of vocabulary used
5 if there are examples of complex sentences.

A

Which jobs are the most important to our society today? I believe that of the five jobs mentioned, these three are of the utmost importance: a doctor, a teacher and a journalist.

First of all, I would like to say that just one doctor can make a big difference to the well-being of the inhabitants of a village or town. Let me give you an example. In the past, people were reliant on witch doctors or wise women. Nowadays, thanks to doctors, we all have access to better diagnosis and treatment.

Teachers are also important to our society. If there is no access to education, then a society will remain in the dark ages. People need to learn and understand about themselves and the way that the Earth works. One example is the education of women. It is a well-known fact that when women are educated, the whole of society benefits, as the women will pass their knowledge down to their children.

Finally, I am going to consider the role of journalists in society. A good journalist will find out as much as possible about things which may affect society — for good or bad. Without the journalists who investigated the Watergate affair, for example, we would never have found out about what Nixon had been doing. Consequently, I believe that journalists are important to society.

To sum up, out of the five professions, I believe that doctors, teachers and journalists are more important to society than engineers or computer programmers.

(250 words)

B

In our society today, most jobs require workers to be computer literate, since businesses are now practically run by computers in order to ensure a faster and more efficient output. Technology is developing and the use of computers is increasing. If one does not know how to work with or even use a computer, it will be very difficult for society. That's why I think that computer programmers are essential to society today.

Secondly, in our society, different jobs provide different experiences. Being a doctor is more important than being a teacher, for example. I know this from my experience. My brother is a doctor in a large hospital in my city and he works very hard and has more money and more respect from society than a teacher. Having respect from society is very important, because if your job is valued, then you feel yourself to be valued as well.

Thirdly, engineers and journalists are quite important but not as important as doctors and computer programmers. In fact, they are often not respected professionals. In many countries, journalists lie and often have to go to jail; consequently, this profession would not be essential to society.

In conclusion, I should add that I would like to be a computer programmer and that is why I think like I do. I will be able to help society with the work I do. The company I am going to work for helps people all over the world to have a much better life.

(251 words)

3 What should the writing plan be for this task?

Introduction ....

Paragraph 1 ....

Paragraph 2 ....

Paragraph 3 ....

Conclusion ....

4 Look at the following words and phrases taken from both essays and try to think of other ways you can say them. (See Writing Folders 3 and 8 in the Student's Book.)

1 First of all, I would like to say that …
2 I believe that …
3 Secondly, …
4 One example is …
5 In conclusion, …
6 important

5 Read this example of an IELTS Task 2 answer and punctuate it (add paragraphing, capital letters, full stops, commas and dashes).

should children be allowed to work that is a good question i believe it depends on the age of the child and the type of work that it is asked to do broadly speaking i think that children under the age of 14 should not be allowed to work but from that age on it is permissible if it is regulated first of all children need to learn about the workplace and the pressures that they will face when they finish school secondly children need to understand the relationship between work and money at a fairly young age unless they are from a very rich family they will need to work one way that many children are introduced to work in my country is by way of a newspaper round or a saturday job another example of how children can be introduced to the world of work is by having work experience weeks at their school this can be a very valuable experience as they need to get up early travel to work deal with people and possibly endure total boredom finally although i believe that children should find out about work when they are teenagers i am totally against children younger than 12 working children need to go to school and they also need to have time to play and grow to sum up i believe that when children reach a certain age it is important that they get a job it is part of growing up of learning to be a responsible adult

6 Write about the following topic. You should make a plan first of all.

> *To get a good job today, it is more important for children to study mathematics and foreign languages than art and music.*
>
> *To what extent do you agree or disagree with this opinion?*
>
> Give reasons for your answer and include any relevant examples from your own knowledge or experience.
>
> Write at least 250 words.

Introduction ....

Paragraph 1 ....

Paragraph 2/3 ....

Conclusion ....

Writing workout 3: Graphs and tables

Academic Training Writing Task 1

1   Which of these are important for a good chart/graph/table task?
    Tick the boxes which apply.

    1   at least 150 words in length ☐
    2   mention of all the data ☐
    3   well-organised paragraphs grouping data ☐
    4   a comparison, if asked for ☐
    5   a repetition of the question ☐
    6   a variety of vocabulary and structure ☐
    7   reasons for any change in the data ☐
    8   accurate figures (possibly approximate) ☐

2   Look at the task below and the sentences on the right. Decide whether or not
    each sentence is appropriate in an answer to the question. If it is not, say why.

The bar chart below shows the amount spent on different types of advertising in the USA in 2003 and 2004. The table shows the six sectors which spent most on advertising in the USA in 2003 and 2004.

Summarise the information by selecting and reporting the main features, and make comparisons where relevant.

Spending on advertising in the USA 2003 and 2004

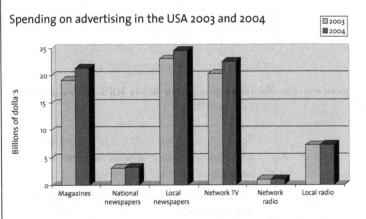

Ranked spending on advertising in the USA in 2003 and 2004

Sector	Rank 2003	Rank 2004
Automotive	1	1
Retail	2	2
Telecom/Internet	3	3
Medicine	4	4
Financial services	6	5
Food, beverages	5	6

---

1   The charts show the amount of money spent by the automotive industry in 2003 and 2004.

2   Food and beverages rose in popularity in 2004 because of the increased power of supermarket advertising.

3   There was an increase in spending on advertising in local newspapers in 2004.

4   I think that local newspapers are the best way to advertise.

5   Although there was a rise in the amount spent on advertising in magazines, there was very little increase in advertising on local radio.

6   There was a dramatic fall in the amount spent on advertising in national newspapers in 2004.

7   The bar chart shows the amount spent on different types of advertising in the USA in 2003 and 2004.

8   The amount spent on advertising in 2004 was just over $20 billion in magazines, under $5 billion in national newspapers, just under $25 billion in local newspapers, around $22 billion on network TV, $1–2 billion on network radio and finally, $6 billion on local radio.

3 Look at the sample answer to the task in exercise 2. Complete the spaces with one of the words from the box.

accounted	change	fell	followed
least	~~overall~~	period	reaching
rose	showed	whereas	

According to the bar chart, there was an **0** ...*overall*... increase in spending on advertising in the USA in the **1** .... 2003 to 2004. Advertisements in magazines, local newspapers and on network TV **2** .... for the largest increases, **3** .... advertising in national newspapers, network radio and local radio only **4** .... a slight increase. The most favoured forms of advertising were in local newspapers, with the amount spent **5** .... almost $25 billion in 2004, **6** .... by network TV at $23 billion. Network radio was the **7** .... favoured form of advertising at $2 billion in 2004.

There was no **8** .... from 2003 in the top four business sectors when it came to spending on advertising in 2004. The automotive industry ranked number 1, followed by the retail industry. Financial services **9** .... to fifth place in the rankings, taking the place of food and beverages, which **10** .... to sixth place.
(160 words)

4 Correct the mistakes below made by IELTS candidates.

1 From this charts, we can find out about the difference in spending between the UK and the USA.
2 The middle chart it show us the increase in money spent in developing countries.
3 The chart describes the amount spend.
4 Britain spent the highest amount in consumer goods.
5 The third most popular goods was toys.
6 Personal stereos were spent nearly the same amount as TVs.
7 The highest popular consumer item was the camera and the lowest was the personal stereo.
8 Majority of people spent most on films.
9 The graph show that electricity use in winter are much greater than in summer.
10 The use of electricity is shown at a pie chart.
11 The number of units decrease sharply.
12 Several figures is increasing.
13 The demand of electricity then decline until 0800.
14 There is a different of 5.2 between the figures.
15 It's clear that unemployment have decreased.

5 Do this Task 1.

The line graph shows changes in car ownership between 1972 and 2002 in the UK. The table shows the main method of travel to work in the UK in 2002.

Write a report for a university lecturer describing the information in the graph and table.

Write at least 150 words.

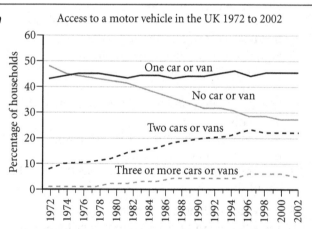

Access to a motor vehicle in the UK 1972 to 2002

Main method of travel to work in the UK, 2002 (% of people)

Country	Car or van	Motorbike or scooter	Bicycle	Bus or coach	Train	Foot	Other
England	70.6	1.3	3	7.5	6.8	10.3	0.5
Wales	80.4	–	1.3	4.5	1.1	11.5	–
Scotland	69.6	–	1.7	11.4	2.9	12.5	1.1
Northern Ireland	79.9	–	–	5.0	–	11.4	1.6

Writing workout 4: Style in essays

General Training and Academic Writing Task 2

1 Which of the following would you **not** expect to find in a formal essay?

 a idioms
 b collocations
 c contractions
 d colloquial language / slang
 e very strong personal opinions / aggressive language
 f abbreviations
 g an impersonal style

2 The following sentences all contain errors of style. Say which errors (a–g) from exercise 1 apply to each. There may be more than one.

 EXAMPLE: I am absolutely against the government putting out ads telling me what to do.
 d (colloquial language: *putting out*)
 g (abbreviations: *ads = advertisements*)

 1 People insist on driving gas guzzlers.
 2 The reason global warming is getting worse is because some countries didn't sign the Kyoto agreement.
 3 We'll soon all be freezing to death if the Gulf Stream changes direction.
 4 We should take advantage of the availability of free resources, e.g. waves and wind.
 5 Some people haven't a clue about the consequences of carbon emissions.
 6 It is no good going by bicycle once in a blue moon; you need to be properly committed to alternative transport.
 7 It's really great that the media are giving this problem so much coverage.
 8 Governments should have a get-together to talk about the problems we face.

3 Rewrite the sentences in exercise 2 using the phrases below. You may need to make changes to the rest of the sentence to make it more formal/appropriate.

 a It is clearly beneficial that
 b have little idea about
 c such as
 d cars which use a great deal of fuel
 e suffering from intense cold
 f It can be argued that
 g high-level discussions
 h occasionally

4 Some of the phrases in exercise 3 are collocations.

clearly beneficial
suffer from cold
intense cold
high-level discussions

Using collocations shows you have a good level of English. Complete the sentences below with the following adverbs to form the correct collocation. There may be more than one answer. Use an English-English dictionary to help you.

clearly	densely	dramatically	heavily
inevitably	repeatedly	seriously	wildly

1 The minister was .... criticised for not doing enough to promote alternative energy.
2 The figures for the factory's carbon emissions proved .... inaccurate.
3 The reasons why the oceans are becoming more acidic are not .... understood.
4 Experts have .... warned the government and industry of the effects of using carbon-based fuel.
5 There is no doubt that sea levels will rise ....
6 Our exploitation of oil .... threatens the environment.
7 Some cities will suffer more than others, especially ones which are .... populated.
8 If we continue to drive larger and larger cars, this will .... result in more and more pollution.
9 The prime minister had .... got his facts wrong.
10 I have .... written to the government to complain about what is happening.

5 IELTS candidates often find it difficult to know how to start Task 2. Read this task and decide which of the four introductions below would gain good marks. Give each introduction marks out of 5 and underline any words or phrases which are useful for introductions.

Write about the following topic:

Governments should make more effort to promote alternative sources of energy.
To what extent do you agree or disagree with this opinion?

Give reasons for your answer and include any relevant examples from your own knowledge or experience.

A

There is no doubt that the Earth is beginning to suffer the consequences of pollution. People should make more of an effort to recycle and to use public transport. Also to use different sources of energy.

B

It has been suggested in recent months that the government is not doing enough to promote alternative sources of energy. My personal opinion is that they should promote alternative sources of energy.

C

It has been known for some time now that a move towards sources of energy which are not carbon-based is urgently required to stop the effects of global warming. In my view, there are too few governments who seem to be promoting the use of other types of energy – from wind, wave, solar and nuclear sources.

D

First of all, I would like to say that this is a subject that is often discussed. Something needs to change and change quickly. I am in favour of wind power, and indeed in my country we use it a lot.

6 Write a full answer to the task in exercise 5.
You should write at least 250 words.

Writing workout 5: Writing correctly in essays

General Training and Academic Writing Task 2

1 Read the essay below on role models for young people. Circle the more suitable linking word or phrase in each case.

0 (*Firstly*) / *Well*, what is a good role model? **1** *Actually / In my opinion*, he or she should be hard-working, honest and think of other people besides themselves.
2 *Naturally / Unfortunately*, many sports stars and celebrities do not have these qualities, possibly **3** *because / owing to* these are not the qualities that helped them to become famous in the first place.

4 *There is no doubt that / As a result*, young people today have access to more information about the world than ever before. **5** *Consequently / However*, much of the information in the media is centred on celebrities and sports stars **6** *because / lastly* stories about these people, especially scandal, will sell newspapers **7** *but / or* make people watch television. **8** *Whereas / Although* much of what young people see or hear is very negative, I believe that most of them are aware that they do not have to copy what a celebrity or sports star does, **9** *especially / clearly*
if it is an example of particularly bad behaviour.

10 *Extra / Another* point to consider is that there are many people in the community who would make excellent role models. My teacher, for example, raises money to help give children in poor countries an education.

11 *At the end / To sum up*, I believe that it is not true to say that the only role models young people have are sports stars and celebrities. Young people can think for themselves.
12 *Really / Consequently*, they are able to see that there are people around them who can fulfil the task of role model rather than relying on people who make the headlines.

2 Each sentence contains an incorrect word. Replace it with the correct one. Use an English-English dictionary to help you.

EXAMPLE: Simon studied ~~Economic~~ at university.
Economics

1 The class spent all yesterday practicing for the marathon.
2 Take my advise, choose a sport which is less competitive than tennis.
3 Salaries of sportsmen and women have raised considerably in the last few years.
4 The team will loose next Saturday.
5 The football court was too hard to play on.
6 The total amount of people who support football in this town exceeds 100,000.
7 You need a coach to give you the knowledges you need to succeed at this sport.
8 Most coaches do more harm than benefit when it comes to training.
9 The standard of life in some countries is very low.
10 My personal assumption is that sport plays an important part in daily life.
11 You will have the possibility to speak to him later.
12 Some sportsmen and women earn a good currency from their sport.
13 I saw an advertising for the Olympics last week on TV.
14 The most popular consumer good is the trainer.
15 The learning of computers should begin at school.
16 She studied in an English-speaking ambience.
17 The least popular homework is washing the windows.
18 She took a part-time work at the local sports centre.
19 I hope you have a good travel to the competition.
20 Youth people today love athletics.
21 Where do you buy your cloths?
22 Don't touch the buttons of the computer.
23 I have no choose in the matter.
24 There are quite a few sports exercises available at the centre.

3 IELTS candidates often have problems with prepositions. Correct the preposition in each sentence below.

1 I'm really grateful for everything they did to me at college.
2 During the period of 1989 and 2001, public services declined.
3 My brother is responsible of training in the company.
4 The government will prevent people to getting jobs without a work permit.
5 I haven't seen you from a long time.
6 The goods won't arrive here since the weekend.
7 The magazine is the least effective medium to communicating news.
8 There is a high demand of electricity in the evenings.
9 Through the Olympics in Greece, everything ran smoothly.
10 There was an advertisement of a job at a local restaurant in the paper.
11 Learning about computers should be compulsory on primary school.
12 I look forward for hearing from you soon.

4 Write out the jumbled text in the correct order. The first part is in **bold**.

1 with a computer every day whether
2 there are undoubted benefits to the use of computers,
3 computers at work, in the home, to pay our bills, to buy books
4 **The computer is an important invention and it**
5 although
6 only that, people who
7 or to plan our holidays. We have dealings
8 has had a huge impact on our lives. We use
9 savings could be deleted. Not
10 bank online are more likely to have
11 we know we are doing so or not. However,
12 that, if something goes wrong, our
13 knows that the banks use computers to
14 process transactions. All our accounts are computerised, with the result
15 their accounts hacked into illegally.
16 there are also some drawbacks. In the first place, everybody

Reading module

Advice on tackling the Reading Module

The Reading Module as a whole

- Spend **60 minutes** on the Reading Module, without any breaks.
- Spend no more than **20 minutes** on each passage. If you spend longer on the first one or two, you won't be able to finish the third.
- You must write your answers on the **Answer Sheet** (see page 64). There is no extra time for doing this. You can write on the Question Paper, but make sure you copy your answers accurately onto the Answer Sheet within the 60 minutes.
- Remember that each question gives you **one mark**, so don't spend a long time on a single question.
- As far as possible, give an **answer to every question**.
- Remember that **you don't need to understand every word**.

Each reading passage

- If there is a headings task, it will appear *before* the passage. Read it quickly before reading the passage.
- Read the **title** and spend about **two to three minutes skimming** the passage. **Mark important information**, such as the main point in each paragraph (often in the first sentence of the paragraph). This will help you to find the relevant part of the passage for each task and question. Ignore details.
- **Don't worry** if you find the passage difficult to understand. You'll probably understand more of it when you try to answer the questions.
- Look at the first task. Read the **instructions** (rubric) carefully and **underline important information**, such as the maximum number of words to give. Advice on each task type is given in the Test folders in the Student's Book.
- If you are not sure of an answer, **write possible answers**, then go on to the other questions in that task. When you have finished the task, go back and choose one answer to each question.
- Check that you have followed the instructions, such as giving only one answer or writing no more than three words.
- If you have spent 20 minutes on the task without finishing it, try and give a possible answer to each question.
- If you have written on the Reading Module, copy your answers onto the Answer Sheet before going on to the next passage.

READING PASSAGE 1

*You should spend about 20 minutes on **Questions 1–13***
which are based on Reading Passage 1 below.

Zheng He

The Chinese admiral-explorer of the 15th century

A Zheng He was born around 1371, to a Muslim family in China's southern Yunan Province, just north of Laos. When he was ten years old, he, along with other children, was captured by the army, and three years later he became a servant in the household of the Chinese emperor's fourth son, Prince Zhu Di.

B He proved himself to be an exceptional servant, becoming skilled in the arts of war and diplomacy and serving as an officer of the prince. Zhu Di became emperor in 1402, and a year later, he appointed Zheng He to the high military position of admiral and ordered him to oversee the construction of a Treasure Fleet to explore the seas surrounding China.

C The first Treasure Fleet comprised 62 ships. The four flagships were huge wooden boats, some of the largest ever built in history: they were approximately 120 metres long and 50 metres wide. The fleet assembled at the capital, Nanjing, on the Yangtze River, and included 100-metre-long horse ships that carried nothing but horses, water ships that carried fresh water for the crew, troop transports, supply ships and war ships for offensive and defensive needs. The ships were filled with thousands of tons of goods to trade with others during the voyage. In the autumn of 1405, the fleet set sail with 27,800 men.

D The fleet used the compass – invented in China in the 11th century – for navigation. Marked sticks of incense were burned to measure time. Latitude was determined by monitoring the North Star in the Northern Hemisphere or the Southern Cross in the Southern Hemisphere. The ships of the Treasure Fleet communicated with one another through the use of flags, lanterns, bells, carrier pigeons, gongs and banners.

E The destination of the first voyage of the Treasure Fleet was Calicut, known as a major trading centre on the south-western coast of India. The fleet reached Sri Lanka and India in 1406, and stayed there for several months, carrying on barter and trade. The following spring, the seasonal change in direction of the monsoon winds enabled the ships to sail towards home. On the return voyage, the Treasure Fleet was forced to battle with pirates near Sumatra for several months. Eventually Zheng He's men managed to capture the pirate leader and take him to the Chinese capital Nanjing, where they arrived in 1407.

F A succession of other voyages followed, back to India and Sri Lanka, to the rich city of Hormuz on the Persian Gulf, and along the east coast of Africa, almost as far south as Mozambique. During each of Zheng He's voyages, he encouraged diplomats from other countries to travel to China, either aboard his ships or on their own vessels.

G Emperor Zhu Di died in 1424 and was succeeded by his son Zhu Gaozhi. The new emperor cancelled the voyages of the Treasure Fleets and ordered shipbuilders and sailors to stop their work and return home. Zheng He was appointed military commander of Nanjing.

H The leadership of Zhu Gaozhi did not last long, as he died in 1426 at the age of 26. His son – and Zhu Di's grandson – Zhu Zhanji became emperor. Zhu Zhanji was much more like his grandfather than his father was, and in 1430, he restarted the Treasure Fleet voyages by ordering Zheng He to resume his duties as admiral and make a seventh voyage, in an attempt to restore peaceful relations with the kingdoms of Malacca and Siam. It took a year to gear up for the voyage, which departed as a large expedition with 100 ships and 27,000 men.

I Zheng He is believed to have died in 1433, on the return trip, although others claim that he died in 1435 after the return to China. Nonetheless, the era of exploration for China was soon over, as the following emperors prohibited trade with foreign countries and even the construction of ocean-going vessels, thus ending an era of trade and exploration.

J It seems likely that a detachment of one of Zheng He's fleets, though not the admiral himself, sailed to northern Australia during one of the seven voyages. The evidence lies both in the Chinese artefacts found there and in the oral history of the native Australians.

Questions 1–5

Reading Passage 1 has ten paragraphs labelled **A–J**. Which paragraph contains the following information?

*Write the correct letter **A–J** in boxes 1–5 on your answer sheet.*

1 a summary of journeys to various places
2 examples of equipment used during voyages
3 speculation concerning a possible destination
4 details of the composition of a fleet of ships
5 how the weather affected the timing of a voyage

Questions 6–9

Complete the sentences below with words taken from Reading Passage 1.
*Use **NO MORE THAN TWO WORDS** for each answer.*
Write your answers in boxes 6–9 on your answer sheet.

The first treasure fleet

6 The ships carried a large quantity of .... which were to be sold.
7 The sailors used the night sky to calculate the ships' ....
8 The fleet sailed to an important .... in India.
9 While returning to China, the fleet was attacked by ....

Questions 10–13

*Complete each sentence with the correct ending **A–G** from the box below.*
*Write the correct letter **A–G** in boxes 10–13 on your answer sheet.*

10 Zhu Di ....
11 Zheng He ....
12 Zhu Gaozhi ....
13 Zhu Zhanji ....

A travelled to Australia.
B ended trade with other countries.
C ended the construction of ships.
D took children away from their homes.
E wished to end hostilities between China and certain other countries.
F made contact with foreign diplomats.
G ordered ships to be built.

READING PASSAGE 2

*You should spend about 20 minutes on **Questions 14–27** which are based on Reading Passage 2 on the following pages.*

Questions 14–19

Reading Passage 2 has seven paragraphs **A–G**.

Choose the correct heading for each paragraph from the list of headings below.

*Write the correct number **i–x** in boxes 14–19 on your answer sheet.*

List of Headings
i   The problem of finding jobs
ii   Outsiders begin to interfere
iii A lack of homes
iv   Setting off for a new life
v   The community is broken up
vi   A long period of isolation
vii The impact of tourism on island life
viii A struggle to survive
ix   Work has a different function
x   Asking for help

Example Paragraph **A**	*Answer* vi

14	Paragraph **B**
15	Paragraph **C**
16	Paragraph **D**
17	Paragraph **E**
18	Paragraph **F**
19	Paragraph **G**

The evacuation of St Kilda

A St Kilda is a tiny archipelago at the mercy of the storms of the North Atlantic Ocean. The islands are among the most spectacular in Scotland. But the greatest fascination is that, for over a thousand years, people lived there. Cut off from the mainland for most of their history, the islanders had a distinct way of living their lives, mainly eating the tens of thousands of seabirds that returned year after year to breed on the rocks. Their self-sufficiency meant that throughout their history, they possessed a sense of community that was rare in the modern world.

B The St Kildans led a lonely life. They had more in common with the people of other isolated islands, like Tristan da Cunha, than they ever had with fellow Scots living in the cities of Edinburgh or Glasgow. Isolation had a big effect upon their attitudes and ideas. The people sacrificed themselves year in and year out, in a constant battle to secure a livelihood for themselves and the rest of the community. In such harsh conditions, life was only possible because the whole community worked together.

C For centuries, the world outside ignored the people of St Kilda. They were content on the mainland to allow such a remote community to go its own way. As long as the people of St Kilda were so isolated, they were insulated from the forces that wished them to conform. This changed in the 19th century, when St Kilda was subject to pressures from the rest of the country. Education, organised religion and tourism all attempted to throw into doubt the St Kildans' way of life. Help, as interpreted by the articulate spokesmen of the richer and more advanced society on the mainland, was best given by persuading the islanders to give up the struggle.

D In the early 20th century, the strength of the community became weakened as contact with the rest of Britain increased. When disease decimated their numbers, and wind and sea made it difficult to get adequate supplies of food, the St Kildans were forced to turn to the mainland for assistance. However, many on the British mainland, including the government, believed that agreeing to the St Kildans' requests for a nurse and a postal service would be a waste of money. More fundamentally, it was thought that if the St Kildans could not adapt and accept the values of the dominant society, the only solution was to evacuate the islands.

E In 1930, the St Kildans finally agreed to abandon their homes. They settled on the Scottish mainland, not realising that it meant throwing themselves into the 20th century. As adults, they had to accept those values that most Scots are taught to believe in from birth. For instance, the islanders found it difficult to base their existence upon money. They had never lived in a world in which they bought goods and services from each other. They had, of course, accepted gladly the opportunity of making a little money for themselves at the expense of tourists, but that intrusion had never altered the basic relationship one St Kildan had had with another.

F The islanders showed themselves indifferent to the jobs they were given on the mainland. The labours asked of them were unskilled contrasted with the spectacular feats they had once performed in order to kill seabirds. Moreover, while they had been living on the islands, killing birds had directly provided the community with food to survive. On the mainland, on the other hand, the tasks that they were asked to perform did not provide them immediately with what was needed to keep them fed and warm. There was an intermediate step: employment provided money, which in turn made it possible to purchase the necessities of life.

G The history of the St Kildans after the evacuation, of their inability and lack of resolution to fit into urban society, makes sad reading. If St Kilda had been an isolated home, the islanders were to discover that the remote district of Scotland in which they were settled was even more alien. On St Kilda, at least they had formed a tightly-knit community with a common purpose. When they were resettled on the mainland, the St Kildans were forced to live in homes far apart, in a society whose values were unacceptable, if not incomprehensible, to the majority of them. For many, the move was a tragedy.

Questions 20–22

Choose **THREE** letters **A–H**.
Write your answers in boxes 20–22 on your answer sheet.

Which **THREE** points are made about how people used to live on St Kilda?

A   The chief source of food was found locally.
B   It was essential for people to help each other.
C   Very few people had visited mainland Scotland.
D   The people had a different religion from the majority of Scottish people.
E   The people wanted a more advanced way of life.
F   The homes were unsuitable for modern life.
G   Money played an insignificant role in life.
H   The people disliked visits by tourists.

Questions 23–26

Complete the summary below.
Choose **NO MORE THAN ONE WORD** from the passage for each answer.
Write your answers in boxes 23–26 on your answer sheet.

The twentieth century

In the early 20th century, the islanders had more **23** .... with the rest of Scotland. The number of inhabitants fell because of **24** .... , and bad weather led to shortages of **25** .... Many people on the mainland were unwilling to spend money on a **26** .... or other services for St Kilda.

Question 27

Choose the correct letter, **A, B, C** or **D**.
Write your answer in box 27 on your answer sheet.

Which of the following is the most suitable subtitle for Reading Passage 2?

A   The role of money in modern communities
B   How a community adapted to a different form of life
C   The destruction of an old-fashioned community
D   How a small community resisted government plans

READING PASSAGE 3

*You should spend about 20 minutes on **Questions 28–40** which are based on Reading Passage 3 below.*

The Nature of Language

Language is an extraordinary institution, standing in as much need of explanation as any other aspect of human life, possibly more. But to explain it, one has to stop taking it for granted. Virtually all of us are pretty fluent employers of language; we grow up with it as we grow up with the ability to walk or run, and using it seems as easy as those activities. To see how truly remarkable language is, we must, as the psychologist Wolfgang Köhler put it, retreat to a 'psychic distance' from the subject.

Language is the most complex and sophisticated of our possessions. Only very recently, for instance, have grammarians begun to uncover the enormously complicated rules of grammar which underlie our languages, and they still have a long way to go. Computers can be marvellous at dealing with mathematics and playing chess. Yet, at least at present, no computer is at all close to the reproduction of human verbal abilities. Computers are, at best, second-rate users of language, while animals are not users of language at all.

Talking might be seen as the defining characteristic of human beings. No doubt we are also the only creatures who laugh, and have two legs and no feathers – but that is not too interesting. We may be the only creatures who use tools and who organise politically – and this is more interesting. Still, amongst many peoples, political organisation and the use of tools are extremely rudimentary, whereas all known communities have possessed sophisticated languages. Further, it is probably easier to find analogies in the animal world to tools and politics than it is to language.

Many animals, of course, are capable of producing noises which cause their friends or enemies to respond in certain ways, but these noises are so different in kind from human speech that it is, at best, a misleading analogy to speak of such noises being part of a language. First, animals are incapable of organising their noises into sequences beyond the most primitive level, whereas the most salient characteristic of human talkers is their ability to form an infinite number of sequences from a limited stock of noises. As the poet and critic Herbert Read once remarked, 'no difference between man and beast is more important than syntax'. Second, animals produce their noises in direct response to stimuli in their environment, as when a bird squawks at the approach of a cat. Such noises are analogous to human cries of pain or alarm, not to the sentences we produce. Nothing in my environment 'stimulated' me to write down the sentence I just wrote down. In the light of this, it is easier to understand those followers of the French philosopher René Descartes who found it impossible to suppose that animals could be capable of any mental activity. 'If beasts reasoned,' said one of them, 'they would be capable of true speech with its infinite variety.' We might not want to go as far as that, but at least we must admit that speech is one, if not *the*, salient feature of human nature which distinguishes it from any other sort of nature.

Not only is language our most sophisticated, important and unique possession, it is also, remarkably enough, an almost universal human possession. As already mentioned, all known human societies have possessed a language, whatever else each of them may have lacked. Not only that, but whereas there are mathematical geniuses and chess-playing geniuses, when it comes to language, nearly all of us are capable of producing and understanding an infinite number of sentences.

Language is also remarkable in its versatility. By uttering the appropriate noises, in the right circumstances, a single person in a single day can easily do each of the following: inform others of what is happening, ask them to do something, command them, excite them, promise them, insult them, express anger and get married. As some of these examples show, we do not in general utter noises as an activity separate from other activities. We perform actions with words, actions which it would be difficult, inconvenient or even impossible to perform without words. The number of such possible actions is indefinitely large.

Questions 28–33

Do the following statements reflect the claims of the writer in Reading Passage 3?

In boxes 28–33 on your answer sheet write

YES if the statement reflects the claims of the writer
NO if the statement contradicts the claims of the writer
NOT GIVEN if it is impossible to say what the writer thinks about this

28 Grammarians now have a thorough understanding of their subject.
29 Even the least developed communities have complex languages.
30 Certain noises that animals make can be classified as language.
31 Certain human cries have something in common with animal communication.
32 People who are good mathematicians are likely to be good at chess.
33 Talking usually forms part of a wider activity.

Questions 34–37

Complete the notes below.
*Choose **NO MORE THAN ONE WORD** from the passage for each answer.*
Write your answers in boxes 34–37 on your answer sheet.

Characteristics of human beings:
- unlike animals, able to use language and to **34** ....
- far more capable than animals of manipulating **35** .... and organising politically

Characteristics of animals:
- cannot create **36** .... of noises
- only make sounds in reaction to **37** ....

Questions 38–40

Look at the following people (Questions 38–40) and the list of claims below.
Match each person with the claim credited to them.
*Write the correct letter **A–F** on your answer sheet.*

38 Herbert Read
39 Wolfgang Köhler
40 a follower of Descartes

List of Claims

A Attempts to understand the nature of language require objectivity.
B Computers will soon use language as skilfully as human beings.
C More than anything else, grammar distinguishes human beings from animals.
D Speaking can be compared with physical activities such as walking.
E The inability of animals to speak shows that they are unable to think.
F There is no limit to what human beings can say.

Are you: Female? ⊂⊃   Male? ⊂⊃

Your first language code: ▶ 0 1 2 3 4 5 6 7 8 9
   ▶ 0 1 2 3 4 5 6 7 8 9
   ▶ 0 1 2 3 4 5 6 7 8 9

IELTS Reading Answer Sheet

Module taken (shade one box):   Academic ⊂⊃   General Training ⊂⊃

#		✓ ✗	#		✓ ✗
1		1	21		21
2		2	22		22
3		3	23		23
4		4	24		24
5		5	25		25
6		6	26		26
7		7	27		27
8		8	28		28
9		9	29		29
10		10	30		30
11		11	31		31
12		12	32		32
13		13	33		33
14		14	34		34
15		15	35		35
16		16	36		36
17		17	37		37
18		18	38		38
19		19	39		39
20		20	40		40

Checker's Initials	Marker's Initials	Band Score	Reading Total

Acknowledgements

The authors would like to thank Catriona Watson-Brown for her helpful suggestions and careful editing.

Thanks also go to Annabel Marriott at Cambridge University Press for her constant diligence and support, and to Stephanie White at Kamae for her creative design solutions.

The authors and publishers would like to thank the teachers and consultants who commented on the material:

Australia: Stephen Heap; Brunei: Caroline Brandt; Spain: Chris Turner; Taiwan: Daniel Sansoni; United Arab Emirates: Paul Rawcliffe; UK: Jan Farndale, Roger Scott, Rob Shaw, Clare West

The authors and publishers are grateful to the following for permission to reproduce copyright material. It has not always been possible to identify the sources of all the material used or to contact the copyright holders and in such cases the publishers would welcome information from the copyright owners.
Apologies are expressed for any omissions.

p. 4: *The Times* for article 'N'Kisi the parrot knows what he's talking about', 27 January 2004, by Lewis Smith, © NI Syndication; p. 6: Adapted excerpts from 'The Rituals of Dinner' by Margaret Visser (© 2002 by Margaret Visser) are reproduced by permission of PFD New York; p. 14: Oliver Burkeman for adapted article 'Wear your genes to work' from *The Guardian*, 3 November 1999; p. 19: Bill Giduz for adapted article, 'Looking back down the street' from *Juggler's World*, Vol. 42, No. 2; p. 22: HowStuffWorks. com for adapted text 'How Skyscrapers Work' by Tom Harris taken from www.howstuffworks.com; pp. 24–25: BBC World for adapted text from www.bbc.co.uk/nature; p. 30: Philip Ball for text based on *Bright Earth*, Penguin Books, 2001. By permission of Penguin Group Ltd; p. 38: Ken Haley for the adapted article 'Pole vaulter' from *The Guardian*, 9 December, 2000; p. 42: Australian Government for the adapted text 'Welcome to New South Wales' taken from http://www.immi.gove.au/settle/booklets/text.nsw/eng. pdf, copyright Commonwealth of Australia, reproduced by permission; p. 59: HarperCollins for the text adapted from 'The life and death of St Kilda' by Tom Steel. Reprinted by permission of HarperCollins Publishers Ltd. © Tom Steel, 1988; pp. 61–62: Adapted text from *Philosophy and the Nature of Language*, David E. Cooper, 1973. Pearson Education Limited, © Pearson Education. All rights reserved.

The publishers would like to thank the following people for permission to reproduce copyright photographs:

CORBIS/© Cuchi White p. 8 (br), /© Roger Ressmeyer p. 20, /© Greg Fiume/NewSport p. 52 (cl); © Salvador Dalí, Gala-Salvador Dalí Foundation, DACS, London 2005. 'The Persistence of Memory', 1931 (oil on canvas) by Dalí, Salvador (1904–89) Museum of Modern Art, New York, USA/Bridgeman Art Library, London p. 36; Getty Images/ Robert Harding World Imagery/R H Productions p. 34 (c), /The Image Bank/Theo Allofs p. 24 (r), /The Image Bank/Jerry Driendl p. 34 (r), /The Image Bank/Siqui Sanchez p. 51 (c), /© David Paul Morris p. 16 (l), /Photodisc/Ryan McVay p. 34 (l), /Photographer's Choice/Peter Dazeley p. 6, Photographer's Choice/Stuart Dee p. 8 (bl), /Photographer's Choice/Andreas Stirnberg p. 19, /Photographer's Choice/ Adam Jones p. 22, /Photographer's Choice/Lester Lefkowitz p. 51 (l), /Jeff Reinking/NBAE p. 18, /Stone/Robert Frerck p. 8 (tr), /Stone/Art Wolfe p. 38, /Stone/Tim Fach p. 42 (l), /Stone/Ben Edwards p. 46 (tr), /Stone/Jon Gray p. 46 (tl), /Stone/Shuji Kobayashi p. 46 (lcr), /Taxi/Ron Chapple p. 46 (br); © Aimee Morgana p. 4; Railphotolibrary. com/© W A Sharman p. 16 (r); Rex Features/© The Travel Library p. 8 (tl), /©BEI p. 14, /© Dave Penman p. 40, /© Matt Baron/BEI p. 52 (l), /© Nils Jorgensen p. 52 (cr), /© Andrew Couldridge p. 52 (r);
© Science Photo Library p. 24 (l); Superstock p. 10, /© age fotostock pp. 29, p. 46 (ucr), /© Bridgeman Art Library, London p. 31, /© Super Stock p. 42 (r), /© Prisma p. 51 (r).

The publishers are grateful to the following illustrators:

Mark Draisey: pp. 27, 44; Kamae Design: pp. 12 (t), 13, 20, 23, 41, 43; Gillian Martin: pp. 7, 12 (b), 28

Key: l = left, r = right, c = centre, t = top, b = bottom

The publishers are grateful to the following contributors:

Catriona Watson-Brown: editorial work
Hilary Fletcher: photographic direction, picture research

CPSIA information can be obtained
at www.ICGtesting.com
Printed in the USA
LVOW04s0147031217
558381LV00006B/99/P